Most books on online marketing are neith
This is both. Two huge likeable thumbs u

~ **Dave Kerpen**, *New*
Likeable S

A practical guide for CEOs looking to master marketing on the web. Adam and Toby have written a simple, no-fluff book as well as thrown in 33 templates to implement (and supercharge) your marketing today.

~ **Verne Harnish**, author of *Mastering The Rockefeller Habits*
and CEO of Gazelles

Adam Franklin and Toby Jenkins are the new power duo of digital marketing. Their how-to guide *Web Marketing that Works* is a powerful blueprint packed with concrete insights and practical tools that will multiply your team's success.

~ **Liz Wiseman**, best-selling author of *Multipliers*

In *Web Marketing that Works*, you will learn everything you need to know to generate attention for your business. Just like my two friends Adam and Toby, the book is fun, approachable, slightly alternative, and it delivers great ideas about how to develop strategies and implement tactics for success.

~ **David Meerman Scott**, best-selling author of
The New Rules of Marketing & PR

Is there a 'one-size fits all' strategy for brands to better understand the new myriad of ways that they can connect a message with a consumer? Adam and Toby think so. In *Web Marketing that Works*, you are given a real and practical how-to guide to get your business more digitally savvy. A lot of books on the market speak to the 'why' this is so critical for business success today. This books speaks to the 'how'…and it's something that every business needs to know and do.

~ **Mitch Joel**, author of *Six Pixels of Separation* and *CTRL ALT Delete*
and President of Twist Image

The problem with new marketing is that practitioners look for the easy route. They either copy other companies or leave it to their agencies to come up with ideas. Relationships between your business and your customers are just that ... they're yours. Adam and Toby help you become the success story that others want to copy.

> ~ **Brian Solis**, digital analyst and author of
> *What's the Future of Business (WTF)*

Adam and Toby deliver on the irresistible offer: a mother lode of ideas grounded in experience and insight, and focused templates to custom fit those ideas to your business.

> ~ **Liz Strauss**, business strategist and author of *The Secret to*
> *Writing a Successful and Outstanding Blog*

With comprehensive coverage, exceptional detail, and dozens of free templates, this is the most useful book on digital marketing ever. It's years worth of knowledge and insights packed into a couple of hundred pages. Indispensable, and a must-read!

> ~ **Jay Baer**, *New York Times* best-selling author of *Youtility*:
> *Why Smart Marketing is About Help not Hype*

Adam and Toby have put together a commendable and rare treat for those seeking to learn web marketing: a book that is both comprehensive AND easy to digest. By taking complex topics and boiling them down to their essence, the pair have made critical information on everything from SEO to blogging to social media and beyond accessible to everyone.

> ~ **Rand Fishkin**, Moz founder and author of
> *Inbound Marketing & SEO*

No 'pie-in-the-sky' theories with this book. *Web Marketing that Works* is 100 per cent actionable, includes dozens of easy-to-use templates and is built for marketers at the biggest brands to the one-person start up.

> ~ **Joe Pulizzi**, author of *Epic Content Marketing* and
> founder of Content Marketing Institute

The web has changed marketing forever! Now buyers—not sellers—are in control. Adam and Toby's book gives you the marketing framework for business today so that you're using the web to empower buyers at their four decisive moments.

~ **Robert Bloom**, author of *The New Experts* and *The Inside Advantage* and US Chairman/CEO of Publicis Worldwide

Adam and Toby have created an important resource for marketers, perfect for entrepreneurs and enterprise alike. This well-written volume provides coverage of a number of critical web marketing issues and an elegant journey from strategy to tactics not commonly covered in most introductory marketing books. If you want to drive leads, you owe it to yourself to read this book.

~ **Eric Keiles**, co-author of *Reality Marketing Revolution* and *Fire Your Sales Team Today*

The team at Bluewire Media has created a practical, actionable guide to help businesses launch, manage and measure their inbound marketing efforts, including insights from their experience, templates to keep efforts organized and efficient, and best practices to guide your lead generation efforts. You won't want to miss it.

~ **Brian Halligan,** author of *Inbound Marketing* and CEO of Hubspot

If you want to be on the bleeding edge of marketing, this book is for you. *Web Marketing that Works* throws out yesterday's strategies and provides a roadmap for how to win in web marketing TODAY. EntrepreneurOnFire will be implementing these strategies, and I can't wait for the results!

~ **John Lee Dumas**, host of *Entrepreneur On Fire*, the #1 iTunes business podcast

Adam and Toby 'get it'. I have seen them in action and they understand how the social web works and how to make results happen. This book shows you how to succeed with your marketing online!

~ **Jeff Bullas**, author of the Amazon bestseller, *Blogging the Smart Way* and *Forbes* Top 50 Social Media Power Influencer (#11)

Adam and Toby are the real deal. They are passionate about how web marketing can help business owners. This book is packed with practical advice and truly useful examples. A must-read for business owners. I devoured every page.

~ **Valerie Khoo**, author of *Power Stories*

If you are serious about moving your online marketing forward then Adam and Toby are the genuine article. Experts walking thriftily, delivering results for business owners!

~ **Brett Kelly**, author of *Business Owner Wisdom* and
CEO of Kelly+Partners

Wow! That's all I can say. I've seen my fair share of books claiming to share the secret sauce of web marketing, but none of them have even come close to this. Adam and Toby really know their onions, and this book is full of practical examples, how-tos, and step-by-step instructions. It's the perfect guide for anyone who's just setting up their own business. For that matter, I think most established businesses could learn a lot from it too. I know I did, and I've been in the game since 2001! Well done, boys.

~ **Glenn Murray**, author of *SEO Secrets* and *Practical SEO Copywriting*

A great read for any small business owner, overwhelmed by theory, who simply wants to take action. We are who Google says we are. That's just how it is. *Web Marketing that Works* will ensure the reader (who actions these tested ideas) sees an ROI from their marketing efforts that they deserve. It's less a book, more a hardened battle plan.

~ **Tim Reid**, host of *The Small Business Big Marketing Show*,
Australia's #1 marketing podcast

Adam and Toby have combined some of the best marketing lessons and resources into a straightforward book that both makes the case for why and then gives step-by-step instructions on how to do it right. They humbly share their mistakes, then they give insights into their secrets for results. It's a great example of itself: content that drives relevance and results. I recommend this book for marketers in virtually any industry. You'll read it in a weekend and refer back to it (and the templates it contains) over and over again.

~ **Andy Crestodina**, author of *Content Chemistry*

For most of us, web marketing is a big, scary puzzle. We avoid it because we're terrified of stuffing up, or we pay 'experts' a fortune and don't even know if it's working. After reading this book full of practical advice and templates that are truly idiot-proof (trust me!) you will let out a huge sigh of relief and think: 'I can do this. And I can start TODAY!'

~ **Marty Wilson**, best-selling author of the *What I Wish I Knew* series

Adam and Toby have the runs on the board—this book is seriously jam-packed with stories, tips and practical ideas that will help your brand stand out in today's noisy marketplace.

~ **Trevor Young**, author of *microDOMINATION*

It's time to put an end to lousy web marketing advice and that is exactly what Adam Franklin and Toby Jenkins have done in *Web Marketing that Works*. If you want real advice, street smart advice and practical advice, from two of the most experienced in the game, this is the book you really need to read.

~ **Andrew Griffiths**, Australia's #1 small business author

If you want to get into the trenches and make a real impact with your online marketing, learn from Adam Franklin and Toby Jenkins. They have gained mastery through doing, and in *Web Marketing that Works* they share the nitty-gritty of precisely what you need to do to get the results you want.

~ **Ross Dawson**, futurist and author of *Living Networks*

As a serial entrepreneur operating 8 businesses, 3 of those online and in different countries, I thought we knew a lot about web marketing. From this book I've picked up a stack of ideas and processes that will clearly work a treat for us. THANK YOU Adam and Toby. Clear, concise and logical. They cover the different aspects of web marketing, by story telling and with great process tips and templates. This book is going to become compulsory reading for all my senior management team and everyone near me involved in marketing. It's brilliant to get us all on the same page and to help us strategise a new marketing plan to suit us. Congratulations—in practical web and feeder marketing, you guys rock.

~ **Mike O'Hagan**, serial entrepreneur and owner/founder of MiniMovers

I highly recommend *Web Marketing that Works* to marketing managers and those responsible for an organisation's digital strategy. After surveying the marketplace for a robust conceptual and practical framework for creating and managing a web and social media activity, nothing else comes close to this. I am delighted to see this model now in print. It will become the benchmark framework for 'thinking marketers' to deliver superior client and business outcomes. It really is essential reading.

~ **Peter Bowman**, author of *Service 7*

Adam and Toby have laid out a clear, easy-to-follow process that allows businesses to build genuine relationships with their customers. This is a great resource for entrepreneurs who are new to the online marketing world and are stuck between conflicting advice about online marketing.

~ **Danny Iny**, author of *Engagement from Scratch!*

Most general marketing books are incomplete and lack practical application. This is a comprehensive primer that every business should read and apply. Now they can thanks to Adam and Toby's sharing of their own marketing laboratory. Take this book and go to market!

~ **Kevin Daum**, best-selling author of *ROAR! Get Heard in the Sales and Marketing Jungle* and *Video Marketing For Dummies*

WebMarketing
THAT WORKS

WebMarketing
THAT WORKS

Confessions from the
Marketing Trenches

ADAM FRANKLIN & TOBY JENKINS

WILEY

First published in 2014 by John Wiley & Sons Australia, Ltd
42 McDougall St, Milton Qld 4064

Office also in Melbourne

Typeset in 11/13.5 pt ITC Berkeley Oldstyle Std

© Adam Franklin & Toby Jenkins Partnership 2014

The moral rights of the authors have been asserted

National Library of Australia Cataloguing-in-Publication data:

Author:	Franklin, Adam, author.
	Other Authors: Jenkins, Toby, author.
Title:	Web Marketing that Works: confessions from the marketing trenches / Adam Franklin and Toby Jenkins.
ISBN:	9780730309277 (pbk)
	9780730309307 (ebook)
Notes:	Includes index.
Subjects:	Internet marketing.
	Electronic commerce.
	Internet advertising.
	Online social networks – Economic aspects.
	Success in business.
Dewey Number:	658.872

Cover design by Peter Reardon, www.pipelinedesign.com.au

Printed in Singapore by C.O.S. Printers Pte Ltd

10 9 8 7 6 5 4 3 2 1

Disclaimer
The material in this publication is of the nature of general comment only, and does not represent professional advice. It is not intended to provide specific guidance for particular circumstances and it should not be relied on as the basis for any decision to take action or not take action on any matter which it covers. Readers should obtain professional advice where appropriate, before making any such decision. To the maximum extent permitted by law, the authors and publisher disclaim all responsibility and liability to any person, arising directly or indirectly from any person taking or not taking action based on the information in this publication.

For our families and for Luce.

Contents

Foreword by David Meerman Scott

What we all really want is ATTENTION

Entrepreneurs, CEOs, and business owners want people to pay attention to their company. Marketers, PR pros, advertisers and salespeople are on the payroll for one reason: *To generate attention.*

In thinking about attention, there seem to be four main ways to generate it today.

You can *buy* attention. This is called advertising.

You buy access to people through expensive television commercials, magazine and newspaper ads, the Yellow Pages, billboards, tradeshow floor space, direct mail lists and the like.

Advertising agency staffers are really good at buying attention. The problem is that whenever you have an attention problem and consult an advertising agency, the solution always involves buying attention.

You can *beg* for attention. This is called public relations.

You beg for access via the editorial gatekeepers at radio and TV stations, magazines, newspapers, trade journals and, more and more these days, bloggers, podcasters and people with followings on other social networking sites.

I realise that the word 'beg' is a little extreme, but in my former life as VP of corporate communications at several different global companies, I did feel a bit like a beggar. And these days I get hundreds of pitches a month from people (usually PR agency staffers) who want me to write about something on my blog or in my books or to pimp them on Twitter and frankly, many of these pitches have a whiff of desperation about them.

Public relations agency staffers are really good at begging for attention. The problem is that whenever you have an attention problem and consult a public relations agency, the solution always involves generating attention from third parties.

You can *bug* people one at a time to get attention. This is called sales.

You knock on doors, call people on the telephone, send personal emails, or wait for individuals to walk into your showroom.

Again, sorry about the extreme nature of the word 'bug' but that's how I feel when confronted with pushy hardcore sales tactics.

Salespeople are really good at getting attention one person at a time. The problem is that whenever you have an attention problem and consult a sales professional, the solution always involves generating attention one person at a time.

You can *earn* attention online.

This idea is quite simple. You create something interesting and publish it online for free: A YouTube video, blog, research report, series of photos, Twitter or Instagram stream, e-book, Facebook page and the like.

And guess what? You can earn attention for your business yourself!

There's no doubt that *earning* attention works best. Why? Because today, buyers are in charge! Referencing blogs, social networks, review sites and other web-based tools, they often bypass the traditional marketing and selling model altogether—learning for themselves about your products and services, your competitors, and what your customers say about you (whether true or not!).

Don't struggle to adjust to this new environment—be agile and master it. The key is a real-time mindset and an arsenal of new communication tools. You win hearts and minds by creating low-cost (and no-cost!), measurable strategies and tactics that help buyers you don't yet know discover you. Publishing content online is free or nearly free. YouTube? Free. Twitter? Free. You don't have to pay to generate attention!

The best organisations have become content publishers and information brokers—communicating by delivering the precise information that buyers need at just the right time and in just the right way.

In fact, this idea of how to generate attention is so simple that it can be summed up like this: *On the web, you are what you publish.* If you're publishing great information on the web, you are great and people will find you and want to do business with you. If you're publishing nothing on the web, then you're nothing, nada, and nobody will find you when they search for a company like yours. And if you're publishing crap, well, then … you get the idea.

Organisations gain credibility and loyalty with buyers through content, and smart organisations think and act like publishers in order to create and deliver content targeted directly at their audience.

Don't push product. Teach people something. Share your expertise.

More than five years ago I met Adam and Toby, which is remarkable because I live in Boston and they are 10 000 miles away in Sydney. How did we meet? On the web of course! We shared many of the same philosophies about how to generate attention in today's hyper-connected world.

Soon after, we shared a meal in Sydney and cooked up a plan. They had been working on a strategy document for their clients and shared their draft with me. Our ideas were so similar that we collaborated on publishing what became our Web Strategy Planning Template that we would jointly brand and share with our followers (you'll learn about it in these pages). And boy, am I glad I did that because it's now been seen by more than a quarter of a million people! Imagine that? A simple PDF document that helps hundreds of thousands of people to become better at how they generate attention and it cost zero to publish.

In *Web Marketing that Works*, you will learn everything you need to know to generate attention for your business. Just like my two friends Adam and Toby, the book is fun, approachable, slightly alternative, and it delivers great ideas about how to develop strategies and implement tactics for success.

Good luck as you embark on generating attention for your business.

And remember, on the web, you are what you publish.

David Meerman Scott

Best-selling author of ten books including The New Rules of Marketing & PR, *now in its fourth edition with more than 300 000 copies sold in English and available in over 25 languages, from Bulgarian to Vietnamese.*

Boston, MA

January, 2014

About the authors

Adam Franklin and Toby Jenkins founded Bluewire Media in 2005 and help clients with their web marketing. They provide workshops, events, online courses, consulting, mentoring, keynote speaking and also form joint ventures.

Adam Franklin is an **international social media speaker** and marketing manager of Bluewire Media. Adam is a regular writer for **StartupSmart** and occasionally contributes to SmartCompany, *Sydney Morning Herald* and radio station **2UE**.

Toby Jenkins is CEO of Bluewire Media, a business speaker and also competed at the **Athens Olympics** as part of the Australian water polo team.

Their Bluewire Media blog has been named in the **Top 20 Australian Business Blogs** every year since 2010, and their weekly Bluewire News email goes out to over 10 000 subscribers. They also host a podcast called **Web Marketing That Works**.

Adam and Toby co-created the **Web Strategy Planning Template** which has been seen by hundreds of thousands of people worldwide. They have featured on **Smart Company's Hot 30 Under 30** and the **Dynamic Business 2010 Young Guns** lists of young entrepreneurs, as well as in David Meerman Scott's bestselling book *The New Rules of Marketing & PR*.

Adam and Toby have been mates since Grade One. They went to primary school, high school and university together, competed in water polo and swimming teams, travelled overseas and then decided to start a business together in 2005.

Bluewire Media

Blog: www.bluewiremedia.com.au/blog
Twitter: @Bluewire_Media
Facebook: www.facebook.com/BluewireMedia

Adam Franklin

Twitter: @Franklin_Adam
LinkedIn: www.linkedin.com/in/adamfranklin
Personal blog: www.adamfranklin.com.au
Email: adam.franklin@bluewiremedia.com.au

Toby Jenkins

Twitter @Toby_Jenkins
LinkedIn: www.linkedin.com/in/tobyjenkins
Personal blog: www.tobyjenkins.com.au
Email: toby.jenkins@bluewiremedia.com.au

Acknowledgements and thanks

We would like to thank the following people who have shaped our business, our marketing and this book. Many have guided us via their blogs, podcasts, speaking, books and videos, and a few we have the privilege of knowing and calling friends. Thank you.

Amy Porterfield
Amanda Gonzalez
Andrew Griffiths
Andy Crestodina
Ann Handley
Anne Sorensen
Ash Richardson
Barry Feldman
Ben Richardson
Bernie Borges
Bob Bloom
Bob Ruffolo
Brett Kelly
Brian Clark
Brian Halligan
Brian Solis
CC Chapman
Charles Badenach
Chris Brogan
Chris Guillebeau
Clay Collins
Cliff Ravenscraft
Corbett Barr
Dan Norris
Dan Zarrella

Daniel Pink
Danny Iny
Darren Rowse
Dave Kerpen
Dave Peck
David Graham
David Greiner
David Heinemeier Hansson
David Koch
David Meerman Scott
David Siteman Garland
David Smerdon
Dean Jackson
Derek Halpern
Dharmesh Shah
Doug Kessler
Eric Keiles
Eric Reis
Erik Qualman
Erika Napoletano
Evan Fortune
Gary Bertwistle
Gary Vaynerchuk
Giam Swiegers
Gina Lofaro

Gini Dietrich
Glenn Murray
Georgina Dent
Guy Kawasaki
Iggy Pintado
Jack Daly
Jaime Tardy
James Adonis
James Shramko
Jared Easley
Jared Spool
Jason Falls
Jason Fried
Jay Abraham
Jay Baer
Jeff Bullas
Jen Bishop
Jeremiah Owyang
Jess Whittaker
Jill Konrath
Jim Collins
Jim Stewart
Joe Polish
Joe Pulizzi
Joel Flom

John Fison
John Jantsch
John Lee Dumas
Jon Morrow
Jonathan Crossfield
Julien Smith
Karen Beattie
Keith Ferrazzi
Kevin Daum
Kevin Ryan
Kylie Bartlett
Lance Schwab
Larry Bloch
Laura Fitton
Laurel Papworth
Lee Odden
Leo Widrich
Liz Strauss
Liz Wiseman
Llew Jury
Malcolm Turnbull
Malcolm Burrows
Malcolm Gladwell
Marc Lehmann
Marcus Childs
Marcus Sheridan
Mari Smith
Mark Parker
Mark Schaefer
Marshall Goldsmith
Marty Wilson
Mathew Myers
Matthew Johnson
Matt Crawford

Melissa Jun Rowley
Mel Kettle
Matt Crawford
Melissa Jun Rowley
Mel Kettle
Mia Freedman
Michael Hyatt
Michael Stelzner
Mike Cannon-Brookes
Mike Lieberman
Mike O'Hagan
Mitch Joel
Nancy Duarte
Naomi Simson
Nassim Nicholas Taleb
Nick Bowditch
Nick Kellet
Nigel Heyn
Oli Gardner
Pat Flynn
Patrick Lencioni
Paul Wallbank
Peter Blasina
Peter Bowman
Peter Diamandis
Peter Williams
Ramsay Taplin
Ray Edwards
Rand Fishkin
Robert Cialdini
Robert Rose
Ron Baker
Ross Dawson
Ryan Holiday

Sally Hogshead
Scott Belsky
Scott Berkun
Scott Dinsmore
Scott Farquar
Scott Ginsberg
Scott Stratten
Seth Godin
Sharon Williams
Shayne Tilley
Simon Kalinowski
Siimon Reynolds
Simon Sinek
Sonia Simone
Steve Krug
Susan Cain
Tamar Weinberg
Ted Rubin
Tiffany Sauder
Timothy Ferriss
Tim Martin
Timbo Reid
Tom Poland
Tony Hollingsworth
Trent Dyrsmid
Trevor Young
Tristan White
Valerie Khoo
Vanessa Fox
Verne Harnish
Vivienne Storey
Will Swayne
Yaro Starak

We'd like to say a huge thank you:

To the Bluewire community for sharing in this nine-year journey with us so far.

To Valerie and Georgie, and Kristen, Alice, Elizabeth, Keira, Jem and the team at Wiley for making this book a reality.

To Greg, David, Mike, Toni, Tony, John and Ash for helping us navigate our business adventure.

To the Bluewire team for your friendship and your help in creating, implementing and refining so much of what we've shared in this book.

To our friends and families who have supported us since the beginning. Especially Frannie and Marg who helped us 'bash these words into submission'.

And to Lucy, the love of Toby's life.

First and foremost: our story and why you need this book

A journey of a thousand miles begins with a single step.

Lao-tzu

January 7, 2005, was an auspicious day for us. We walked out of the business licensing office in Spring Hill, Brisbane, into a sweltering Australian summer day. We'd just registered our trading name, Bluewire Media. We were officially business owners. All that was missing was one small piece of the puzzle—clients.

And so began our marketing journey.

Here we were, non-technical business owners who'd never written a line of code, selling websites. Rather than learning how to program, our passion was in learning how to market, run and grow a business. We knew marketing was a key ingredient and we needed to learn how to get leads for our burgeoning business.

Door knocking was our opening move. Armed with notepads, matching business shirts and a polished script, we started canvassing the local businesses.

'Hi. My name is Adam and this is Toby. We're from Bluewire Media, a web design company. We were wondering if you needed a website?'

'No thanks, not at the moment.'

'No problem. Thanks for your time.'

And so it went. We pounded the pavement for an entire two days, working our way through store after store, business after business, in the summer heat. The result? Nothing. Not a single solitary lead.

The breaking point came when it was Toby's turn to lead. He accidentally followed the script verbatim: 'Hi, I'm Adam ...'! We realised our gaffe, left the store and burst into laughter. It was either that or cry. We needed to look for a better way.

We graduated from door knocking to cold-calling. At least now we were in the shade. We had a brainwave and started to qualify businesses that were advertising in the *Brisbane News* magazine but didn't have a website. Clearly they had a marketing budget, so all we had to do was convince them to spend it with us.

There were three things hurting our credibility. Firstly, we were selling websites while our own was still under construction. Secondly, we had no website portfolio, since we had no clients. And thirdly, when we were making the calls, the birds in the trees beside Adam's parents' deck were chirping loudly in the background.

To make up for these chinks in our armour, we stepped up our sophistication and trialled our first offer: we'd mock up a website design for the business if they would agree to a meeting. While this was labour intensive, it won us the attention we were after and we started to book some appointments.

Interestingly, though, our first sale came through word-of-mouth, from an old water polo coach. His mate at the pub said he needed a website. Our coach passed on his details and we landed the gig. Receiving our first-ever cheque for a deposit of $247.10 is still one of our favourite business memories.

And we progressed. We learned two things from that first win: that our community was valuable and that we needed to deliver value. So we tapped into our existing networks, such as our university alumni and old boys' networks, and drummed up any PR we could off the back of Toby's recent performance at the Athens Olympics. All of our early press mentions featured water polo caps and laptops—anything to spread the Bluewire word!

We signed up to a free listing in the Yellow Pages and were seen at every networking function possible. We'd show up at the opening of an envelope if given half a chance.

We came to realise that the old adage that word-of-mouth is the best form of marketing was absolutely true. Since all of our business was coming through our networks and relationships, we decided that would be where we invested our time, money and resources. As a start-up, we had no money to invest in paid advertising so we focused on growing and nurturing our network by being generous and offering advice, and this led to sales.

Marketing on the web was fantastic for this because it scaled. Anybody on the web could potentially find us through our website, and with the click of a button we could send an email to our entire network. This was the birth of our Bluewire News emails. With these breakthroughs, our business, Bluewire Media, was off and racing.

We soon learned that the best use for the Yellow Pages was as a step for Adam to stand on so he was a bit taller in photos next to Toby. We loved the web and were hooked on this new business so threw ourselves into reading books, listening to CDs (it was pre iTunes!), attending conferences and learning from marketers online to discover all we could about web marketing that works.

We furiously implemented what we learned, experimenting and testing as we went. As non-technical first-time business owners, we were brimming with enthusiasm, and it's been like that for nearly a decade now. This book is the product and culmination of our firsthand experiences as we've tried to find the most effective ways to market our business on the web.

On the shoulders of giants

From the outset, our love of business, marketing and the web inevitably put us on a happy collision course with the work of David Meerman Scott, Seth Godin, Chris Brogan, Julien Smith, Gary Vaynerchuk, Brian Halligan and Dharmesh Shah.

Back in the mid to late 2000s these were the people who shaped our thinking about marketing a business in today's connected web world. Destiny for us was the ground-breaking ideas in their blogs and books about permission marketing, inbound marketing, the 'new rules' and building trust.

Everything totally resonated and the timing was perfect. These people validated what we had been experiencing and, better yet, they provided a framework and language that went with it. The world was on the cusp of a genuine revolution. And as entrepreneurs in a web business, we were free to implement the ideas unhindered.

We had an 'aha!' moment seeing David Meerman Scott's keynote presentation called 'The New Rules of Marketing & PR' via satellite in Sydney. Wow! It stopped us in our tracks. You cannot beg, bug or buy attention, David argued. You must earn it by publishing great content on the web. He was speaking our language, even though he'd just opened our eyes and ears to it. What perfect timing to cross paths with David's ideas and have the luxury of being able to start implementing them straight away.

The old rules of marketing from the pre-web days dictated that you must beg (press releases), bug (salespeople) or buy (ads) people's attention. Today these approaches don't work as well as they used to. Now you must earn attention by publishing content on the web that solves your buyers' problems. In David Meerman Scott's words, 'on the web you are what you publish!'

Around the same time, we read Seth Godin's *Permission Marketing*. His message—that you can't interrupt people with advertising messages and expect them to listen—also rang true. You can't beat people over the head, online or offline. You need their permission, and remarkable content is the ticket. Seth had even called out the offending style of marketing and given it a name—interruption marketing. This idea resonated with us, clearly delineating fundamentally different marketing styles. We knew interruption marketing wasn't for us.

Chris Brogan and Julien Smith's book *Trust Agents* and Gary Vaynerchuk's *Crush It!* provided a blueprint for taking action, based on the idea that being human, earning trust and developing relationships one at a time were the keys to success on the web. Very powerful and so simple.

Brian Halligan and Dharmesh Shah's book *Inbound Marketing* provided the final piece of the puzzle, a marketing philosophy to live by and a name for it too—inbound marketing. Attract visitors with great information, continue to nurture these people by helping and teaching them, and eventually they will become paying customers and delighted referrers.

Advertising no longer reigned supreme

In our early days, advertising agencies reigned supreme in the marketing world. As a small web firm, we partnered with many of them and worked with their clients, although we found from the very start that advertising principles simply didn't seem to perform the same when applied to the web. Banner ads, splash pages and flash intros were not things that we enjoyed personally, and it never seemed right to subject other people to them.

The stop-start campaign mentality didn't sit well with us either. Three to six months of frenzied activity followed by a complete halt seemed an unlikely formula for lasting success. Surely we were in this for the long run? Still, it was work, it paid the bills for our start-up, and it allowed us to cut our teeth in business and marketing.

A universe of connected humans

It turned out we weren't the only ones who didn't really like advertising and its unwelcome interruptions. The marketing world had changed to a place where we could all block out ads through do-not-call lists; TiVo; pop-up blockers; unsubscribe, un-follow and un-like buttons; and simply clicking out of a website. You could no longer effectively interrupt your way into people's lives. And if you did manage to intrude, you'd be more likely to annoy them than encourage them.

Instead you need to draw people in with inbound marketing. Use blogs, social media and content to be discovered, attract leads and win customers. Also, the stop-start campaign mentality doesn't apply — inbound marketing is an ongoing program. We need to stop creating interruptions to insert into other people's content, and start creating the content ourselves.

There is a supreme irony in the fact that the *most* modern technology is a vehicle for the development of a universe of real, connected human beings. The key to success now, more than ever, is to be human — to earn trust and develop relationships with other human beings.

The future is now

The permission-based world that Seth Godin describes in *Permission Marketing* has already arrived. What happens next is up to us.

We're living in an age when we can be connected to anyone on Earth with WiFi and a smartphone — a supercomputer in our pocket with more capability than was thought possible even 10 years ago.

Consider how we've changed over the past decade, since we started our business. We now carry mobile devices, and neither of our homes has a landline. We are fully mobile with our laptops, and our desktop computers have been recycled. We use email but never send faxes. We Google for information and never open the Yellow Pages. Our prized CD collections have become relics made obsolete first by iTunes and again by Spotify. Toby has bought the lion's share of his books on Kindle rather than in paperback. We keep our photos on Facebook, not in hard-copy photo albums. We buy online using PayPal or credit card and have never used a chequebook. We get our news online, rather than buying newspapers. Adam doesn't own a TV, nor do we watch commercial TV, but we have paid to download shows like *Homeland*.

Marketing has changed just as much.

Why you need this book

If you own, run or market a business, if you are a corporate marketing exec or work in a marketing firm, if you are looking to start a company or start your career, or even if you are still a student with these aspirations, then these are the skills you need to acquire. You'll be able to deliver results and leapfrog over your peers who aren't willing to make the shift to the web. If you've got enough skin in the game, and want it badly enough, this book will work for you.

The good news is it's quite simple, although certainly not easy. You need to love what you do and you need to care. You need to love the people you touch with your marketing and care about solving their problems. If you don't truly care, then inbound marketing won't be your thing.

But you do care, or you wouldn't be reading this book.

Remember, each part of your web marketing plan is a building block that contributes to the whole. You'll understand how each of the parts fits together, whether it be social media, search, email marketing, website or blogging. You have the luxury of focusing on one area, shipping it and then focusing on a new one. It's like going to the gym: you work on a new muscle, let it recover and then make it stronger next week. Once you've gradually worked your way around all your muscles you'll be in great shape!

Everything in this book is implementable. The templates and tools we offer, all of which can be downloaded free from our website, are exactly those we use ourselves and with our own clients.

Why listen to us?

Since starting Bluewire Media in January 2005, we've been in the trenches implementing strategies, learning and improving web marketing for our clients and ourselves.

For the best part of a decade our business has been on the frontline of web marketing. We've digested hundreds of books, thousands of blog articles and countless presentations on marketing, the web and business, and we've been putting it all into practice. All up we have invested over 10 000 hours and we've put the best parts of this experience into this book and into the library of free tools and templates you can download and use for yourself.

We've built a marketing pipeline and inbound flow of leads—5617 last year, a total unmatched by any international Hubspot partner. We advise listed companies, speak around the world, run workshops, deliver online courses, partner with businesses and communicate with more than 10 000 subscribers every week through our Bluewire News emails.

Now you can learn from us and fast-track your own marketing journey. Everything we share with you is from our firsthand experience. Whether it's about blogging, social networks, landing pages, email marketing, search optimisation or web design, we've been adapting as the technology changes, keeping up in the rapidly changing world of marketing.

Are you still with us?

We hope so. If you're ready to grow your community and build a web platform, but you're not sure exactly what you need to do, that's great—because we're about to take the first steps with you.

When reading this book you can follow the old-school path of cover to cover, but that isn't necessary. We suggest you check the contents page and dive into any specific area you want, then download the associated templates and start implementing. Then move ahead to your next area of focus. Seasoned web marketing professionals might choose to scan through the book for the Pro Tips. Skip straight to these for instant hits of value.

As you work your way through the different sections, your web universe will take shape and you'll be building a web marketing asset that will pay dividends for years to come.

We are confident that if you implement even half of what you read in this book you will be setting your business and your career up for a great future. Use the book as a guide for your own actions, come back to it and tweak the ideas to suit your own taste and circumstances. Let us know how it goes. We would love your feedback and look forward to hearing about your own experiences. You can reach us at:

adam.franklin@bluewiremedia.com.au

toby.jenkins@bluewiremedia.com.au

Let's begin.

Bonus 33 free templates

Download all 33 templates at once at:
www.bluewiremedia.com.au/web-marketing-that-works-book

	Template	Ch	URL
1	Web Strategy Planning Template	1	www.bluewiremedia.com.au/web-strategy-planning-template
2	Inbound Marketing Methodology	1	www.bluewiremedia.com.au/inbound-marketing-methodology
3	Content Marketing Sales Funnel	4	www.bluewiremedia.com.au/content-marketing-sales-funnel
4	Web Marketing Health Check Template	5	www.bluewiremedia.com.au/web-marketing-health-check-template
5	Web Marketing Report Template	5	www.bluewiremedia.com.au/web-marketing-report-template
6	Website Content Collaboration Template	6	www.bluewiremedia.com.au/website-content-collaboration-template
7	Website Checklist for Graphic Designers	6	www.bluewiremedia.com.au/website-checklist-for-graphic-designers
8	Communication Schedule Template	6	www.bluewiremedia.com.au/communication-schedule-template
9	Landing Page Design Template	7	www.bluewiremedia.com.au/landing-page-design-template
10	Lead Nurturing Template	8	www.bluewiremedia.com.au/lead-nurturing-template
11	Blog Post Planning Template	9	www.bluewiremedia.com.au/blog-post-planning-template

(continued)

	Template	Ch	URL
12	Content Marketing Promotion Template	9	www.bluewiremedia.com.au/content-marketing-promotion-template
13	Skype Interview Template	10	www.bluewiremedia.com.au/skype-interview-template
14	Instagram 5 Min Marketing Plan	10	www.bluewiremedia.com.au/instagram-daily-marketing-plan
15	Pinterest 5 Min Marketing Plan	10	www.bluewiremedia.com.au/pinterest-daily-marketing-plan
16	Content Ideas Generation Template	11	www.bluewiremedia.com.au/content-ideas-generation-template
17	Content Publishing Rhythm Template	11	www.bluewiremedia.com.au/content-publishing-rhythm-template
18	Editorial Calendar Template	11	www.bluewiremedia.com.au/editorial-calendar-template
19	SEO Planning Template	12	www.bluewiremedia.com.au/seo-planning-template
20	Google+ 5 Min Marketing Plan	12	www.bluewiremedia.com.au/google-plus-marketing-plan
21	Aspirational Contacts Template	13	www.bluewiremedia.com.au/aspirational-contacts-template
22	Blogger Outreach Email Template	13	www.bluewiremedia.com.au/blogger-outreach-email-template
23	Event Marketing Template	14	www.bluewiremedia.com.au/event-marketing-template
24	Speakers Social Media Template	14	www.bluewiremedia.com.au/speakers-social-media-template
25	Email Sales Copy Template	15	www.bluewiremedia.com.au/email-sales-copy-template
26	Social Media Guidelines Template	16	www.bluewiremedia.com.au/free-social-media-guidelines-template
27	Social Media Planning Template	16	www.bluewiremedia.com.au/social-media-planning-template
28	Social Media Image Sizes Checklist	16	www.bluewiremedia.com.au/social-media-image-sizes-checklist
29	LinkedIn 5 Min Marketing Plan	17	www.bluewiremedia.com.au/linkedin-daily-marketing-plan
30	Social Media Corporate Approval Template	18	www.bluewiremedia.com.au/social-media-corporate-approval-template
31	Facebook 5 Min Marketing Plan	18	www.bluewiremedia.com.au/facebook-marketing-plan
32	Twitter Cheat sheet	19	www.bluewiremedia.com.au/twitter-cheat-sheet
33	Twitter 5 Min Marketing Plan	19	www.bluewiremedia.com.au/twitter-marketing-plan

Part I

How it all works

Chapter 1

Your web universe: content, web and inbound marketing

However beautiful the strategy you should occasionally look at results.

Winston Churchill

We were sitting in a bar in North Sydney—it was the only place open after a long day and it was coffees all round. Beer wasn't on the agenda, marketing was.

'Here's our situation. We've reviewed our marketing budget and realised that we are spending $6000 per month on advertising. This is bringing in leads, no doubt. *But*, and here's the thing, we're gradually having to spend more and more to get the same results. It's like an addiction. It takes a little bit more each time to get the same kick, but if we turn off the tap, the leads dry up. We need to make a transition, to find another, more sustainable way to generate leads without leaving us high and dry. Our question is: Can you help?'

Our answer, of course, was 'Yes'. After all, that's what this book is about—building a web marketing asset that will continue to deliver leads on autopilot without paying for ads each time.

But before we dive into the solution, let's have a quick look at a key difference between advertising and inbound marketing.

Advertising depreciates fast.

The value of a print ad diminishes almost instantly. You pay to place your ad in a newspaper or magazine or online and then hope people buy or enquire, or remember you long enough to do so later. After that ad runs, you may win a few customers, which is great, but by the next day the ad is fish-and-chip wrapper.

Because the value of the ad depreciates so quickly, you need another one immediately to replace it and start the cycle again. So you pay again to reach more people.

In stark contrast, web and inbound marketing presents an opportunity for your asset to appreciate, increasing in value over time.

Building a web marketing asset

In April 2013 Adam wrote a blog post titled 'Marketing Experiments: Email content that gets clicked'. The post was live for six months before it was linked to by the popular Buffer blog (see the link at the end of this chapter). This drove a surge of qualified visitors to our own blog. One particular visitor arrived at our blog and read the article, which ended with an offer to download our free Web Strategy Planning Template. In doing so, he happily exchanged his name and email address and opted in to receive further communications from us. He received our Bluewire News emails for three months before enquiring to see how he could engage our services. He's approved our proposal and will become a client. All initiated from one blog post six months before.

One block at a time

On the web, you are able to build your marketing asset one block at a time. Start with your website, create a flagship piece of content you'll become known for, add a blog, an email newsletter, some guest blogging and social media, and you will gradually assemble the pieces of the puzzle to dominate your niche. As you publish great content and communicate with your audience, they will get to know, like and trust you. With trust, the right customers will gravitate to your organisation and will put their hand up to do business with you, just as in the story above. This is inbound marketing in action.

Web marketing appreciates over time.

That 'Marketing Experiments' blog post Adam wrote six months ago is worth more now than when it went live. When first published it had no views, no backlinks, no comments and no social shares. As time passed, however, people read it and left insightful comments, which added value to the content. People shared it via social networks, and the more tweets and likes it generated, the more this 'social proof' made it appealing to the next reader. And it was being shared with new networks. When some people found the blog post useful they linked to it from their blogs, which introduced a new wave of readers, and the backlink boosted the post in Google's rankings.

Web marketing pays dividends too.

This blog post continues to attract new readers, and a percentage of these readers take Adam up on his offer at the end of the post and download our flagship content. In exchange for this content download, they happily give him their name and email address. Having these new people opt-in to receive more content from us is where the real value lies. They can get to know, like and trust us, which is the only way your marketing will lead to customers and dollars.

As you build up your content, your web marketing asset will increase in value and pay dividends in the form of leads, customers and revenue. This will give you the confidence to turn off your advertising tap.

Your web universe from 20 000 feet

Let's take a look at how your web universe fits together (see figure 1.1, overleaf).

Figure 1.1: Web Strategy Planning Template

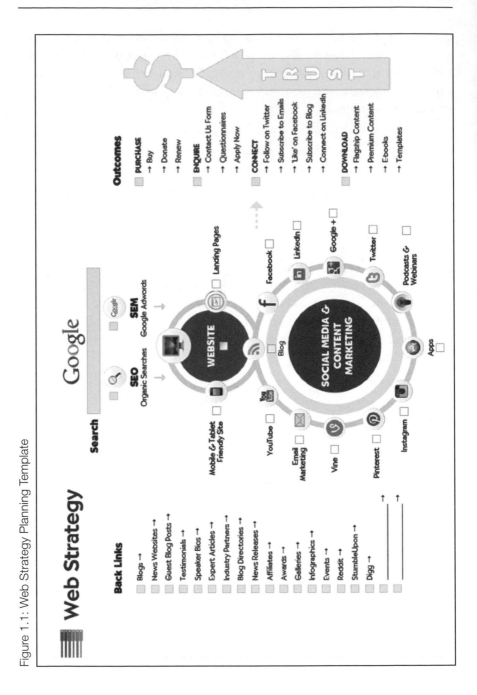

Your website sits right in the centre—it's the hub, where your commercial outcomes take place. Once people arrive at your website, they should be able to identify clearly the journey you would like to take them on. Visitors may choose to take various different paths that suit them, but you need to provide the overall roadmap for their journey. Eventually you want people to be purchasing from you and becoming your customers, but to reach this stage these prospective buyers first need to know, like and trust you.

> ## Pro Tip: Release a piece of flagship content.
>
> The secret to web marketing that works is to release what we call 'flagship' content. It needs to be useful, valuable and genuinely helpful. This will become the cornerstone of your web marketing, something you'll be known for and identified with.

Elements of the web universe

Let's now review the main elements of the web marketer's world.

Trust

Trust is an old concept in marketing. It has always been an integral part of people doing business with people and it's just as important to online marketing. Your web strategy needs to be focused on growing trust with your community. It's about nurturing your customers from knowing you to liking you, to trusting you enough to buy from you when they are ready.

The pathway to increasing levels of trust follows four stages: download (where they get to know you), connect (where they get to like you), enquire (where they get to trust you) and purchase (once they trust you). The eventual commercial goal will be to drive revenue, so let's start with the purchase:

1 *Purchase*. People can buy your product or service—it might be tickets, donations, memberships and renewals, or subscriptions—and become your customers.

2 *Enquire*. Attracting enquiries is one of the primary outcomes of marketing. These might come via forms, phone calls, emails or applications.

3   *Connect.* You may want people to follow you on Twitter, become a fan of your Facebook page or subscribe to your email newsletter. It's all about kicking off a relationship with each member of your community. This will allow you to share further information and to nurture that relationship over time.

4   *Download.* This is where you get people to download your flagship content or other premium content, like e-books, reports and templates—any information you can provide that might begin to help them solve their problem. This is the first step in building trust within your community.

Keeping these outcomes in mind, let's see how the web universe fits together to drive these processes for your business.

Your website

Your site sits in the centre in figure 1.1 for a reason: it's your commercial hub. It's the piece of your web strategy that ties all your efforts together, and it's often where your customers can purchase, enquire, connect and download.

To be successful, a website needs a couple of critical elements that we'll dig into later: landing pages and a blog. It must also be mobile- and tablet-friendly. Because it's where you convert interest into enquiry and dollars, there's a huge amount of value in optimising it and getting it right. Make sure each page is focused on a specific purpose and call-to-action.

There's no point chasing after the latest and greatest in web marketing if you can't convert what you already have!

Once your website is in place and focused on your business outcomes, it's time to explore the options available to you to increase traffic and build your community.

Search

When people search online they overwhelmingly use Google, which splits the results into two: the *organic* results and the *paid* results.

The organic results (the main ones on the left-hand side) are what most people click on. Improving your website's ranking in the organic results is known as *search engine optimisation* (SEO).

The paid results, clearly labelled as ads, are on the right-hand side and often on top of search results. Getting your website listing in the paid results is known as *search engine marketing* (SEM), and Google Adwords is the most common tool for this.

Search engine optimisation

Organic search results might display a page on your website, or an image or video or social media profile (which is why these other aspects of your strategy are also important).

Unpaid or organic search results are the marketer's holy grail — free, highly qualified traffic to your site on a particular search term. You then have the chance to convert users when they click through to your website.

Organic results require good content, time, effort and relationships. Like all good investments, though, once you have a great ranking, you will benefit from it time and again while you work to maintain it. We'll dig into this further in chapter 12.

Search engine marketing

Paid search engine advertising is a qualified source of traffic, but it will vanish when you stop paying. Also, if your keywords become more competitive, you will end up paying more over time. In contrast to organic listings, though, you can get traffic immediately, which may appeal in some circumstances.

Note: We have chosen to focus our efforts on organic search results because they're the ones most people click on, and they contribute to a sustainable marketing asset. We recommend you do too.

Backlinks

Backlinks are literally links back to your website. What purpose do they serve? Firstly, having another web page link to you means people can click through to you. Obviously the more backlinks you get, the more likely people are to find your website.

Secondly, having another website link to yours is seen by Google as a vote of confidence in your content. It is seen as an endorsement and the more of them you can accrue, the higher your page will rank on the search engines.

One thing to note is that not all backlinks are created equal. A backlink from a trusted, authoritative source such as a government, university or news website is worth *much* more than a link from a random, low-quality business directory. We will explore these concepts in more detail later—particularly the importance of nurturing relationships to attract more valuable backlinks.

Social media and content marketing

Another significant way people can find you online is through social media and content marketing. This is the space inhabited by household names like Facebook, Twitter, YouTube, LinkedIn and Google+. This is the glamorous and sexy side of web marketing at the moment (no doubt something new will come along in due course).

And rightly so. Ninety per cent of people trust recommendations from a friend, while only 14 per cent trust advertisements. This means when people mention you or share your content on social media, it will be trusted six times more than anything you say yourself.

Once again it is worth noting here that the search engines increasingly use social media shares (likes, tweets, pins, +1s) to determine their search rankings.

Blog

The final element of the web universe that we haven't yet discussed is your blog.

The best way to look at your blog is as your own publishing platform for your articles, videos and thought leadership. These articles can be found by search engines, linked to by other sites and shared through social media. Your blog also serves to direct people to your flagship content and begins the know, like and trust process.

It's all about building your community.

The more quality content you create, the more people will find you. You'll rank higher on Google, more websites will link back to you and more people will share your content on social media. This creates a positive snowball effect.

As momentum builds, more people are attracted to your blog and website. They can download your flagship content, and connect with you via email and social media. As trust increases, they will eventually enquire and purchase, becoming customers.

Summary

→ Web marketing allows you to build an asset that increases in value and pays dividends (paid advertising, on the other hand, depreciates fast).

→ You can build your asset one piece at a time.

→ Great web marketing helps people to know, like and trust you.

→ Your flagship content is the cornerstone of your web marketing.

→ Your website is the commercial hub of your web marketing.

→ The three main ways people can find your website are via search, backlinks and social media.

→ Quality content snowballs to build momentum and drive your marketing.

Tools and templates

Web Strategy Planning Template
www.bluewiremedia.com.au/web-strategy-planning-template

Inbound Marketing Methodology
www.bluewiremedia.com.au/inbound-marketing-methodology

Buffer blog post
http://blog.bufferapp.com/8-effective-email-strategies-backed-by-research

Part II
Strategy

Chapter 2

Web strategy: defining your buyer personas

Before you ask how, ask who.

Jim Collins

Business and marketing are ultimately about people. Understanding the people in your community will enable you to solve their problems and earn their trust, and will help you achieve your business goals.

Knowing your business goals directs your web strategy. After all, your web marketing efforts must help drive the commercial outcomes. To keep improving you need to track progress against the goals you've set.

Don't start with another marketing activity — start with your buyer.

We first encountered the *buyer persona* concept in David Meerman Scott's *The New Rules of Marketing & PR*, which led us to co-create the Web Strategy Planning Template (see figure 1.1, p. 6). The key distinction between a buyer persona and a target demographic is the focus, not on age, gender or geography, for example, but on *the problems they face*.

Setting your strategy

Setting your strategy is all about understanding your buyer and how you can help them.

So who are you talking to?

You're communicating with real people who just happen to be on their smartphone or at their computer, rather than physically in your shop. Talking to a brick wall or a computer screen is no fun, so it's useful to picture exactly who you want to be chatting or connecting with. Think about what they do, what makes them tick, what problems they face and how you can help them.

That person, your ideal customer, is your buyer persona.

For Bluewire Media, one of our buyer personas is the marketing manager at a mid-size business that is dedicated to being number one in its market niche. She has a supportive IT team and an interested CEO. She wants to increase the number of leads and skill her team up in social media. She is a mid-thirties mum who works four days a week and loves the company of her young family and her girlfriends.

We have named her Nicola.

> ### Pro Tip: Give your buyer persona a name.
>
> Yes, it sounds silly at first, but stay with us. When your buyer persona has a name, they come to life. You can actually picture them and relate to their challenges. This means when you sit down to write content you can write specifically for them. It often helps to have an actual picture so you can see them too, or to base it on a real client.

What are you going to say?

Now you can picture Nicola, it's time to decide what you have to say (that is, the content you are going to publish). The expression 'content is king' was first coined by Bill Gates with reference to the online world. Here's where it rings especially true.

For example, Nicola might like to learn tips about using social media, discover blogging secrets or learn how to set up a Google+ page, so you can plan content that provides that guidance.

The more ideas you can come up with for content that will be helpful to your customers—actual and prospective—the better. Your job then is to take these ideas and start publishing them.

Where are you going to say it?

Author Gary Vaynerchuk extended Bill Gates' maxim to 'content is king and marketing is queen—and the queen rules the household'.

Creating remarkable content with no marketing is like locking Shakespeare in a room to write for himself. In other words, your content is only valuable if people can find it, read it and share it. That's where you need to choose your marketing tools tactically—you have to decide which channels will provide the best fit. The reality is that you don't need to be active on *all* the different channels. Just get started where your buyer personas are.

Building your buyer personas

The back of the Web Strategy Planning Template has space allocated to help flesh out buyer personas. Figure 2.1 shows sections that can easily be used as an activity for you and your team.

Figure 2.1: Web Strategy Planning Template (back)

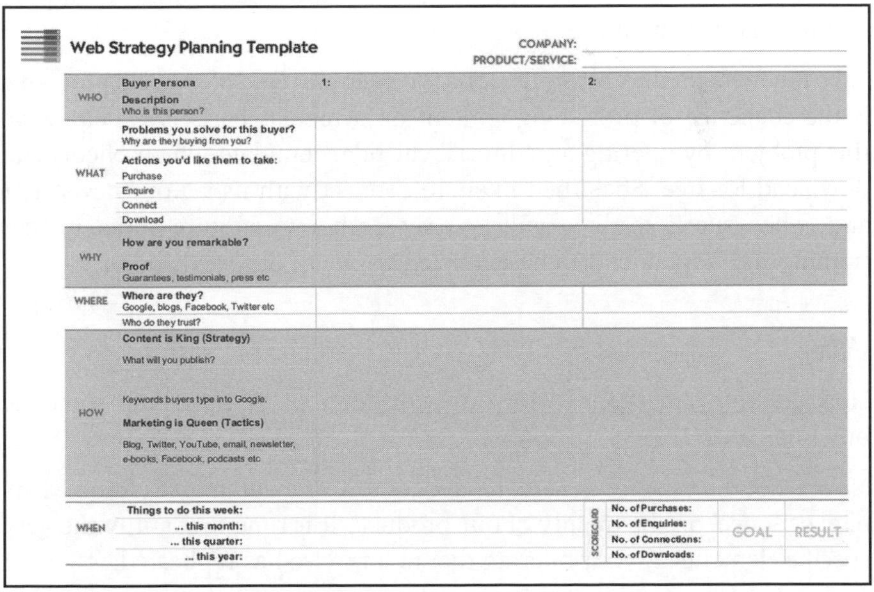

Who

It's all about asking the right questions, and the *who* question is the first and most important. Who are your buyers—professionally, personally? What type of business do they work for? What challenges do they face?

Developing our profile of Nicola obviously doesn't mean that we'll only work with 'Nicolas', but it does serve as a very useful guide for us to identify ideal clients. We named this persona Nicola because at the time we actually had two great clients with that name.

What

The next most important questions revolve around 'What?'

What are the problems that you solve for this buyer persona?

A great starting point is to think through the questions that prospective and existing customers ask you every day. Another way is to consider the most painful challenges you've helped your customers to overcome.

What action do you want them to take?

Building trust at different stages of a buyer's journey means you need to provide them with actions they can take to download, connect, enquire and purchase from you.

Take Bluewire Media's buyer persona for example. One of Nicola's problems is the challenge of producing content on a regular basis. We help solve this problem by offering an editorial calendar template which Nicola can download for free. She's then likely to connect with us via our newsletter and, when she is ready, it will be easy for her to enquire about further training and hopefully purchase a ticket to one of our workshops.

Why

How are you remarkable? How are you different? Why would someone buy from you?

Now is not the time for generic references to 'our great people', 'our *x* years of experience' or 'the quality of our product'. It is time to identify the very specific elements in your offering that no one else has replicated.

For Bluewire Media, our flagship Web Strategy Planning Template, and the tools and templates we offer for download, enable us to distinguish ourselves in a marketplace full of web designers and marketing strategists.

And what proof do you have?

We've built up a portfolio of client testimonials, money-back guarantees, media mentions and the tools themselves, which are all part of our proof.

Other evidence might include recognition, qualifications, results, case studies, endorsements, research, patents, social proof and presentations you've given. There are lots of ways to build up the credentials of your business.

Where

Once you've identified your personas, it's time to go looking for them. Where are they? Think about the groups they hang out with (both online and offline), the events they attend, the social media they use and the memberships they hold.

Where are your '1,000 True Fans'? (See the link at the end of this chapter.)

And, very importantly, who do they trust? What blogs, magazines, websites and media are they reading and being influenced by? Which personalities and thought leaders do they turn to for advice?

For Bluewire, answering these questions led us towards building relationships in business and marketing networks and reaching out to thought leaders and influencers all over the world.

Once you understand *who* your buyer personas are, *what* problems you can solve for them, the actions you want them to take, *why* you're different in their minds and *where* they hang out, you are ready to figure out *how* to reach them.

How

What will you publish for your buyer personas that will help them solve their problems?

There is no shortage of formats to publish your content. For example, you might create blog articles, videos, podcasts, webinars, e-books, email newsletters and infographics. Very often the same content can be repurposed and published in multiple formats.

Understanding what keywords buyers are searching will help you optimise your content for Google. We'll explore all aspects of search in chapter 12.

Just as there are multiple formats in which to publish your content, there are multiple ways to market it. You may distribute your content through your blog, email newsletter, YouTube, Facebook, Twitter, LinkedIn, Instagram, Pinterest or iTunes.

There are so many different ways to reach out to your buyer personas. Ninety per cent of this book is dedicated to the nitty-gritty specifics of how to create content, build a community, reach out to influencers, improve your website, grow your email list and all of the other tactics that will ultimately drive leads and sales for your business.

When

One of the last elements of the Web Strategy Planning Template helps you to set an activity plan for this week, month, quarter and year. We'll address this more specifically throughout the book.

Scorecard

Setting a scorecard to hold you accountable is crucial. Setting goals and tracking your progress against them will help you to refine your strategy and tactics. We'll dig into this more in chapter 5.

We *strongly* recommend doing the buyer personas activity, which is one of the most important elements of this book. When you have a crystal-clear understanding of your buyer persona(s), the tactics laid out in the rest of this book will gain much more traction.

Summary

→ Know your business goals so your web marketing can help you achieve them.

→ Web strategy boils down to understanding your buyer personas and how you can help them.

→ Define your buyer personas by asking:

- Who are they?

- What problems do you solve for them?

- Why will they think you remarkable?

- Where are they and who do they trust?

- How will you publish content and market it to reach them?

→ What actions will you take and when? Set your web marketing goals and track your progress.

Tools and templates

Web Strategy Planning Template
www.bluewiremedia.com.au/web-strategy-planning-template

1,000 True Fans
http://kk.org/thetechnium/archives/2008/03/1000_true_fans.php

Chapter 3

Flagship content: the cornerstone of your web marketing

Stop selling. Start helping.

Zig Ziglar

In our early days, business mentors and peers had raved about Verne Harnish's One-Page Strategic Plan. It was a must-have tool for companies looking to grow. And it was free to download, so we did. Wow! It really delivered and has been the tool that has most shaped our business. Verne's reputation had certainly preceded him, and we wanted to do the same within our community.

Back in 2010, Bluewire Media was just another web design firm. While we prided ourselves on web strategy, we weren't known for it, or anything else. We'd spent years digesting dozens of marketing books and were passionate about delivering a framework to pass on the knowledge we'd gleaned. We wanted our clients to simply 'get it' and be able to take action.

Finding our flagship content: the birth of the template

We spent weeks trying to distill everything we'd learned into a concise tool. It needed to be thorough but not complex or overwhelming, because far too many resources we'd found were confusing even to us, and we lived and breathed this stuff. We scribbled and sketched and started again, until we had something that very loosely resembled a diagram of our web universe. It was a hideous sketch, but after a few days in the hands of our designers it resurfaced looking simplified and sharp (see figure 1.1, p. 6). Small miracles. We showed some clients and some friends and family, and it made sense to them. Bingo!

To give the diagram proper utility, on the flip side of it we created a template for buyer personas to be added. The two sides combined to form the Web Strategy Planning Template. It was heavily based on David Meerman Scott's concept of understanding your buyer personas and publishing content that's useful to them. This template could be filled in by anyone and allow them to fit their entire web strategy onto a single page!

We felt blessed to have learned so much from David Meerman Scott's book *The New Rules of Marketing & PR*, so Toby reached out to him to say thank you, and to show him how he'd influenced our planning template. Here's part of his reply:

> *Toby*
>
> *This is indeed a very interesting strategy plan template. Well done. I really REALLY like it.*
>
> *I would like to suggest that if you were to make the changes that I suggest above and then were to create a co-branded version with my logo and contact info (plus yours), I would be thrilled to blog this (with links to you), use it in my presentations and talk it up during my many speaking engagements.*
>
> *If you want to do this, of course you can use your own version of the template without my logo for your own purposes.*
>
> *What do you say? If you want to go forward, I would ask that you make me a co-branded PDF. I'd send you my logo.*
>
> *Cheers*
>
> *David*

Wow. Not only did we get valuable feedback on how to improve it, but we got the chance to co-create it with David himself. If only David could have seen our two big grins! It was a stroke of luck, a massive thrill and welcome validation that we were on the right path.

The template was to be included in an international bestseller.

A few months later, we received more exciting news from David:

Adam

I am currently writing the third edition of my international bestseller The New Rules of Marketing & PR.

I want to include the template. I will still offer the template as a PDF as we did it. That PDF will be offered in the book too. And I will put a few sentences in the book explaining who you guys are and how we made the template together.

I'm assuming this is cool with you. Can you please confirm?

David

From our collaboration we released the co-branded template under Creative Commons 3.0. (This means anyone can share it with their friends, and even build upon the work, provided it is properly attributed to its original creator. It's a popular way to release content for free but still be recognised.)

It was front and centre on our website, in our email signatures, in our speaker bios, at the end of every blog post, in every social media profile and on every company description.

Every prospective client would be sent it before a meeting, although most were already familiar with it. It was amazing. We were turning up to sales consultations to find that nearly all of the prospects had seen, downloaded or used the template already. Our content had preceded us and had become a stellar point of differentiation.

The template formed the framework of our service offering too.

The Web Strategy Planning Template painted a very clear picture of what clients needed to consider, and it also ensured their whole marketing team was on the same page, literally. It resonated with exactly the marketing managers and business owners we wanted as clients, and very soon we found we were beginning our consulting sessions by helping clients document their strategy using the template.

We built on the IP in the template and packaged it into our paid digital products, our DIY Web Strategy Toolkit and our Web Marketing That Works online course, which we made available on our website. It also formed the basis of our consulting and marketing workshops. It really did transform what we did as a company.

Content so valuable people would pay for it

The Web Strategy Planning Template is a very valuable tool, and perhaps we could have charged for it, but we chose to give it away instead.

Pro Tip: Give away what feels like too much.

This benchmark is really the best way to judge the merit of your content. As we like to advise clients: if it feels like you are giving away too much, then you're probably delivering the right amount of value! In the words of Jay Baer: 'You should aim to give away content that has so much value that people would pay for it if you asked them.'

We released the Web Strategy Planning Template over four years ago, and it has been the single most effective thing we've done in our marketing. It has attracted thousands of new leads and email subscribers, has helped us land our biggest clients and has led to international speaking engagements. The template has helped tens of thousands of people around the world. The many thank-you emails we've received from grateful marketers have highlighted how effective it's been.

Flagship content is your secret sauce!

'Signal versus Noise' is a concept that applies perfectly to the web (it's also the apt name of the popular blog by 37signals). There is a great deal of noise on the web, but truly valuable flagship content releases a powerful signal that cuts through it to raise your business's visibility.

On the web, *better* always beats *more*. Spend the time to create a strong 'signal' rather than churning out bland 'noise'.

Your entire web marketing effort hinges on your flagship content because it gives teeth to everything else you do. Without it, you will find it much harder to gain traction, and that's why we've placed it near the front of the book.

So what should you release as your flagship content? Good question. Start with the rule of thumb that it needs to be so valuable that people would pay for it, or perhaps they already pay for it. In the interest of not making extra work for you (we're already busy enough, right?), first consider what content you already have.

> ### Pro Tip: Release IP you already have.
>
> In deciding on your flagship content, consider first what you already use with prospects and clients. You probably have some very useful tools that you use behind closed doors. They might be on your server, in your drawer or in your head, but if you search around you're sure to uncover a valuable piece that you can call your flagship content.

Conduct a content audit

Sit down with your team, and see what goldmines you are sitting on. Perhaps you have market reports, industry survey results or e-books that you share with clients and prospects. You may have a video of a keynote presentation or market insights from your CEO, or it may be a template, diagnostic tool, booklet, checklist, agenda or training manual. Or consider the following:

- Do you have checklists, templates, guides or calendars that you use with clients?

- Is there a presentation you are well known for?

- Do you have blog posts or interviews that could contribute to an e-book?

If you can identify something unique and special of proven value to your customers, that is what you should release as your flagship content.

Often people are daunted by the task of creating original content, but nearly always the best first move is to find out what you *already have*! Our clients commonly come to recognise the value of some kind of resource they use in their initial dealings with prospective or actual clients.

Why would I give away my intellectual property (IP)?

Most people in your industry will have very similar knowledge and approaches. A customer therefore will hear much the same story from you as they would from a competitor. However, if *you* publish the industry IP first, in the customer's eyes you'll be elevated to the thought leader. If your competition released something similar afterwards, they would be regarded as merely emulating you.

Can I give away too much?

Many people fret over this, when there is no need to. As a rule of thumb, we advocate giving away about 90 per cent of your content for free. Yes, at first this sounds terrifying. *But* if you don't, your competitors will. At some point, *everyone* is out of their depth. Then they will turn to the people they already know, like and trust. By this stage, you're already the authority in their eyes, so who are they most likely to do business with?

In our experience, the more we have given away, the more people have bought from us.

Zappos CEO Tony Hsieh said anyone can copy his website, products and suppliers, or even try to pinch his staff, but no one can copy his culture. We've always embraced his mindset at Bluewire Media.

Yes, a few companies have copied our Web Strategy Planning Template and claimed it as their own (without attribution). That doesn't worry us, though; we know imitation is the sincerest form of flattery.

It can feel counter-intuitive and confronting the first time you release your flagship content, but for us the benefits have well and truly outweighed the negatives. Of course, it's got to sit comfortably with you, but we strongly urge you to consider giving away something that is valuable.

Creating more: premium content

We'd be surprised if you weren't already sitting on your flagship piece of content, and hopefully you've had this 'aha!' moment. Once you've decided on this, there is plenty more premium content you can choose to release too. For the sake of clarity, we refer to your single best piece of content as your 'flagship' and all your other valuable stuff as 'premium content'.

After our Web Strategy Planning Template, we wrote a free e-book called *Web Strategy Secrets* that explains the template in greater detail. We also created the Social Media Planning Template, the Social Media Guidelines Template and the Editorial Calendar Template.

We now have a library of 33 free templates that you will encounter in this book and can access via our website at www.bluewiremedia.com.au/web -marketing-that-works-book.

The reality is that the more you can help your community of customers, prospects and friends, the more they will like and trust you!

Summary

→ Your flagship content needs to be IP that is so valuable someone would be prepared to pay for it.

→ It is probably a piece of IP you have, and use, already.

→ Do a content audit to uncover it.

→ Release your flagship content under Creative Commons so it can be freely shared while you are still recognised as its creator.

Tools and templates

Web Strategy Planning Template
www.bluewiremedia.com.au/web-strategy-planning-template

Social Media Planning Template
www.bluewiremedia.com.au/social-media-planning-template

Social Media Guidelines Checklist
www.bluewiremedia.com.au/free-social-media-guidelines-template

Editorial Calendar Template
www.bluewiremedia.com.au/editorial-calendar-template

DIY Web Strategy Toolkit
www.bluewiremedia.com.au/diy-web-strategy-toolkit

Web Marketing That Works online course
www.bluewiremedia.com.au/web-marketing-that-works-online-course

Verne Harnish's One-Page Strategic Plan
www.gazelles.com/strategy-onepage-strategic-plan.html

Creative Commons 3.0
http://creativecommons.org/licenses/by/3.0/us/

Chapter 4

Content marketing: know, like and trust

Make it about them, not about you.

Simon Sinek

Now you understand how the web universe fits together, you've defined your buyer persona and you've uncovered your flagship content, it's time to dive into the specifics of the path people follow to get to know, like and trust you online.

Content marketing is the process of publishing on the web useful, relevant and interesting content that serves your buyers. The aim is to educate, inform and entertain your prospective buyers so that the 'right people' know, like and trust you, and eventually become your customers and referrers.

As a rule of thumb, 75 per cent of web searchers with a problem are looking for information to help solve it, 23 per cent then compare the options they find, and only 2 per cent are actually ready to take action by enquiring or purchasing. This knowledge has helped us to frame our web marketing efforts and structure our content to guide and assist people at every step of their journey.

Relationships take time

Too often you'll see websites where the only call-to-action is to 'contact us' or 'buy now'. They skip the get-to-know-you stages and expect to close a customer on their first visit. It's equivalent to proposing marriage to a stranger rather than first asking for their phone number. Even if you're the right match for each other, it still takes time for the relationship to develop. On the web, plenty of useful content means people can be comfortable getting to know you at their own pace.

The content marketing sales funnel shown in figure 4.1 helps us understand the trust journey we need to take people on.

Figure 4.1: the content marketing sales funnel

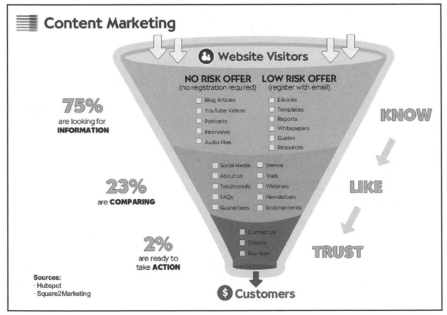

What do you have to offer?

Mike Lieberman and Eric Keiles, in their book *Reality Marketing Revolution*, introduced us to the concept of no-risk and low-risk offers, and we've applied this to the marketing funnel in figure 4.1. Let's take a closer look.

No-risk offers

'No risk' means exactly that: visitors to your site can find the information they are looking for easily and without encountering any barriers.

With more than 500 posts and over 100 videos freely accessible on our blog, there are plenty of ways for people to get to know us. The information includes marketing advice, expert interviews, how-to articles and videos aimed at addressing a wide range of problems.

Low-risk offers

Visitors can access our flagship and premium content in order to deepen their knowledge and to get to know us better. When people are ready, they can easily download our premium content by entering basic details such as their name and email address. We deliver the premium content and reciprocate the gesture of trust by providing our personal details too.

It's known as a low-risk offer because both parties are sharing something of value. This mutual deepening of the relationship is like exchanging business cards when you meet someone interesting. From here the relationship has the opportunity to evolve.

Comparison

At the comparison stage customers conclude that you or your competitors can help solve their problem. They want to make the right decision so they are now comparing options.

So you need to make it as easy as possible for them to decide if you are a good fit for one another. To help this comparison, the more you can share on guarantees, testimonials, frequently asked questions, endorsements and your products and services, the better.

Email newsletters and social media are particularly powerful at this stage in helping them get to know you as people — to humanise your organisation.

This is a crucial part of the customer journey.

Commercial offers

Only after progressing through the first two stages will people be ready to take action. Whether you want this final 2 per cent to call you, contact you via a form or buy now online, make sure it is as easy as possible for them to do so.

Are results really coming?

Yes. The biggest mistake that would-be content marketers make is giving up just before they start to get traction. Content has a compounding effect, just like money in the bank. The more money you have, the more interest it pays you. The more content you publish, the more 'interest' you'll gain from readers, as recognised by social shares, backlinks, search rankings and leads. Just as money you invest today will pay dividends in the future, content you create, publish and share today will earn you leads, customers and revenue for years to come.

The art of repurposing

In addition to the compounding effect, repurposing content enables you to provide multiple formats for your customers, so they can access it their way. Some people prefer to watch videos, some like to read, some like to listen and others simply love infographics.

For example, we have video interviews with Liz Strauss, Darren Rowse, Valerie Khoo, Glenn Murray and Jonathan Crossfield. Each of these was posted on our YouTube channel and embedded on our blog along with a transcript. We then compiled these five interviews into an e-book, which we emailed to our subscribers and published on Slideshare. And of course each of these formats was shared through our social networks.

In other examples we've repurposed premium content into infographics in order to make the content more appealing to visual people. The content can then travel further than it would in one format alone.

So if you've gone to the effort of creating content, leveraging it into different formats can amplify your results.

A final note on etiquette

In the same way that being polite and respectful is important in the real world, it is imperative on the web. For example, always give credit where it's due. This includes providing proper attribution by linking appropriately to people's websites and blog articles.

It all serves to cement your relationships with the people who you interact with on the web.

Summary

→ Give people plenty of content so they can get to know, like and trust you.

→ Seventy-five per cent of web users with a problem are looking for no-risk (for example, blog posts) and low-risk (for example, flagship content) sources of information to solve it.

→ Twenty-three per cent of people compare options, so provide them with product and service information, and testimonials or endorsements. Let them get to know you via email newsletters and social media.

→ Two per cent of people actually take action, so make it easy for them to enquire or purchase.

→ Content has a compounding effect, like money in the bank.

→ Repurpose content to amplify your results.

→ It's always good etiquette to give credit where credit is due.

Tools and templates

Content Marketing Sales Funnel
www.bluewiremedia.com.au/content-marketing-sales-funnel

How to Blog for Business e-book
www.bluewiremedia.com.au/how-to-blog-for-business-e-book

Reality Marketing Revolution by Mike Lieberman and Eric Keiles

Part III

Building home base

Chapter 5

Web marketing metrics and reporting ROI

Not everything that can be counted counts, and not everything that counts can be counted.

Albert Einstein

One metric we checked every day during the earlier years at Bluewire Media was our Google ranking for 'web design Brisbane'. This seemed like the logical search term since we were a Brisbane web design company. After bouncing around the rankings for a few months we settled in third place before rising to number one after six months. We were proud of this achievement.

And yet something wasn't quite right. We weren't getting the kind of leads we'd hoped for. Most of them were comparing prices and looking for the cheapest option. Our service offering had evolved from just web design to a more strategic approach and the leads we were attracting simply weren't the right fit.

However, there was one search term that was consistently delivering top quality leads. That term was 'social media speaker'.

A company looking for a speaker was much more interested in strategic advice than in kicking tyres. These people appreciated our approach, which often led to long-term partnerships as opposed to one-off transactions.

In hindsight we were tracking the wrong metric for our buyer persona. This revelation uncovered a much better option. Because we were tracking these metrics through to revenue, we knew how our best customers were finding us.

The purpose of metrics

The purpose of metrics is to help you determine what marketing activity is driving your business goals. It is really easy to get seduced by a vanity metric like being number one for 'web design Brisbane'. But if you discover it doesn't contribute to your business goals, you're better off changing tack.

Understanding metrics helps you make better marketing decisions.

Most importantly, be open to the feedback loop of your business. The only thing worse than getting caught up in vanity metrics is analysis paralysis, where you feel so overwhelmed you measure nothing. To help you avoid that, let's take a look at what metrics we track and why they are meaningful.

Social media community size

This is your total network size, totalling your connections on Facebook, Twitter, LinkedIn, Google+ and any other online communities.

This gives you an understanding of how many people are in your extended community and is the starting point of many of your relationships. You can add this up manually or there are paid tools like Moz and Hubspot that will collect the data for you.

Number of inbound links

These are a good indicator of the quality of your content and the strength of your online relationships. Google also uses inbound links to determine your search ranking. The best tool for tracking these links is Open Site Explorer.

Pro Tip: Claim linking opportunities.

Google your business name and find websites that have mentioned you but haven't linked back to you. Ask if they can link to you. These are opportunities to grow your inbound links.

Number of visitors

More people coming to your site means more people who may get to know you and become leads. Google Analytics tells you this.

Traffic source

Tracking where people are coming from is great if you want to identify what marketing activity is actually bringing people to your site. Again, Google Analytics tells you this.

Conversion rate

This statistic tells you how many visitors to your website are actually taking action—for example, buying products, enquiring or downloading premium content. For lead generation, an overall conversion rate for your website of 2 to 3 per cent is excellent. The conversion rate for a specific landing page of 30 per cent and above is excellent.

You can measure these by setting up your 'Goals' in Google Analytics.

Total number of active email subscribers

This is another indicator of the size of your more active community. If you've got a good-quality piece of flagship content *and* interesting emails, then this 'total number' should be growing.

However, since people often change jobs (and email addresses), email lists decay at about 0.5 per cent a week; also, people unsubscribe at about 0.5 per cent. So you need to be growing your list by more than 1 per cent a week for it to increase in overall size.

We use Campaign Monitor for this, but all email systems will give you this data.

Email open rates and click-through rates

This lets us know how many people are actually reading our emails. We use it to gauge the quality of our subject lines and as an indication of how much our readers trust us.

If you can get your email open rates up above 20 per cent, you are doing really well. Click-through rates over 4 per cent are considered good, but if you link to your premium content, you can knock this out of the park with click-through rates of over 20 per cent.

Sales enquiries

You can measure the number of sales enquiries and their source. These normally lead to proposals or deal opportunities, and you can track these in your CRM (customer relationship management system; we use Highrise).

Business opportunities

The dollar value and quality of business or sales opportunities you have in your pipeline offer important information.

Actual revenue (sales)

You will want to measure the revenue your business generates and track this back to the original source. This way you can measure your return on investment (ROI).

You can track the dollar value in your accounting system (we use Saasu) and trace the source by asking the customer or using more advanced software like Hubspot to discover how they first found you.

We've created a Web Marketing Report Template to track these metrics over time. You can download it from www.bluewiremedia.com.au/ web-marketing-report-template.

Web Marketing Health Check

To set a baseline, we create a Web Marketing Health Check that incorporates many of these metrics. In addition, we include what happens when you search for your business name.

We also run a Red/Blue Test on your home page text by circling in red mentions of *I*, *us*, *our*, *we* or your company name; and circling in blue mentions of *you* or *your*. This helps to assess if your copy is customer focused; the more blues the better. We learned this test from Mike Lieberman and Eric Keiles' book *Reality Marketing Revolution*.

All of these elements set the baseline to compare future results.

Download the template from www.bluewiremedia.com.au/web-marketing -health-check-template.

Google Analytics

This is one of the great free tools you can use to help you track your metrics. To get you started, download five free readymade Google Analytics dashboards from www.bluewiremedia.com.au/blog/2013/08/free-google -analytics-dashboards.

Another great resource is Dan Norris's article 'The Five Best Google Analytics Dashboards for Content Marketers': www.bluewiremedia.com.au/blog/2014/01/google-analytics-reports -content-marketing.

Summary

→ Many free tools are available to help you track the health of your web asset.

→ Make sure your metrics are tracked through to your business goals. Closing the loop is crucial.

→ Understanding metrics helps you make better marketing decisions.

Tools and templates

Web Marketing Health Check Template
www.bluewiremedia.com.au/web-marketing-health-check-template

Web Marketing Report Template
www.bluewiremedia.com.au/web-marketing-report-template

Campaign Monitor
www.campaignmonitor.com

Google Analytics
www.google.com/analytics

Highrise
www.highrisehq.com

Hubspot
www.hubspot.com

Moz Analytics
www.moz.com

Open Site Explorer
www.opensiteexplorer.org

Saasu
www.saasu.com

Five free ready-made Google Analytics dashboards
www.bluewiremedia.com.au/blog/2013/08/free-google-analytics-dashboards

The five Best Google Analytics Reports for Content Marketers
www.bluewiremedia.com.au/blog/2014/01/google-analytics-reports
-content-marketing

Chapter 6

Building your own website

A good plan implemented today is better than
a perfect plan implemented tomorrow.

George Patton

The news arrived from the international marketing conference Inbound13.

Congrats, you won the following: **Most Inbound Leads (International)** —
5,617 New Leads, Most web leads generated! We'll be announcing the
news of your victory at INBOUND13.

This was exciting validation for the hard work we'd put into planning,
improving and marketing our website over the last 12 months. Even
though we couldn't attend the conference in Boston that year, we were
thrilled, because we knew we had overcome the five dreaded traps of web
projects and delivered a project that was producing inbound leads.

But it wasn't just the last 12 months. It was based on everything we'd
learned before that too ...

Setting up our own website

When we sold our first website, we didn't have one ourselves. We needed
something up as soon as possible.

So we bought a template online, added basic contact details, used the logo Toby's brother had created for us and slowly added to the site as we completed projects. It was not pretty, but it was a starting point—people could find us; we existed.

In total we've been through five website redesigns in nine years and succeeding iterations became more sophisticated. Our business needs changed, our understanding of web marketing increased, or the pain of our existing situation drove us to make a change. Often it was all three.

If your website doesn't evolve, it's dead.

A custom-designed website with an email signup form was the second version built by our team. We felt much more professional.

Implementing a content management system followed, which made updates much easier. Then we installed a WordPress blog to allow us to publish articles and publicly share what we'd learned. Always the call-to-action was to contact us—via email or phone. We then progressed to enable people to transact directly on our website via credit card for purchases such as products and event tickets.

Research had shown that 75 per cent of people are looking for information to help solve their problem. This meant that our site needed to be content rich. So in our latest iteration we provided even more useful, educational content for free on our blog. We took it one step further and released more premium content on landing pages to convert the most interested visitors into leads.

For the next 23 per cent of visitors who wanted to compare us to our competitors, we allowed people to get to know us and provided peace of mind via our About Us section, social media profiles, guarantees, testimonials, case studies, portfolio, press and videos.

The final 2 per cent of visitors, ready for a commercial relationship, could easily enquire or purchase.

Tablets and mobile device usage had also exploded. So we needed to build the site in a responsive design format, to allow it to adjust to different screen sizes.

Like the rest of your business and your marketing, your website must continually evolve. Having been on the front lines of web design for nearly a decade we are all too familiar with the ambition-crushing pitfalls that bring website projects to their knees. In that time we've also developed a framework to overcome them.

Five pitfalls of website projects

There is no doubt that your website is a central component of your business's web strategy. Getting it right can be hard work. Time and budget overruns, feature creep (adding features and functionality late in the game), content preparation challenges, getting approvals ... If you've built a website before, then you'd be one of the lucky few if you haven't struck these issues!

For years we battled them. As an excruciating lesson, our worst-ever project took *two years* to go live. That was our lowest point (thank goodness). From there we set out on a journey of discovery to find out how we could turn building websites into a fast, effective, exhilarating experience for our clients and our team.

With every project we tried to improve, to deliver a better service to our clients. We searched high and low for advice on how to deliver better websites, faster. We borrowed ideas from a diverse range of people and industries—not just web designers. After several false starts, we implemented our own system of strategising, defining and managing website projects that ultimately enabled us to deliver them six times faster than before.

In our nine years of planning, designing and building websites, we've made our own mistakes and witnessed horrors that you wouldn't wish on your worst enemy. They have all boiled down to problems in five areas that have consistently broken projects:

1   *Planning*. The old adage that 'failing to plan is planning to fail' is absolutely true for web design projects. You'd never start building a house without a plan. Don't make the same mistake with your website.

2   *Content*. This is the backbone of your site. How it all fits together will dictate your design and technology choices. It is what drives your marketing, social media and search engine ranking. The effort required to create content is often grossly underestimated when building a website.

3   *Design.* Making design decisions can be hard because everyone has an opinion when it comes to visuals. Separating this stage into two areas, layout design and visual design, is crucial to avoiding multiple iterations.

4   *Build.* Adding features and functionality late in the process, known as 'feature creep', can kill a website's timeline and budget. Separating what is mandatory for your site from what can be added later is the only way to deliver a successful project.

5   *Communication.* Waiting for feedback and approvals can also cripple a project. Having a communication plan committed to by all parties will dramatically impact the speed of your project.

What follows will help you plan, execute and manage your website and is based on all the lessons we've learned building hundreds of sites for ourselves and our clients.

Pain #1: Lack of planning

The first steps in a successful website project are determining the strategy, knowing your buyer personas (see chapter 2) and defining the project.

The planning workshop

To paraphrase Seth Godin's advice:

Thrash hard at the start of the project so that the project can run smoothly for its duration.

You need to keep this principle in mind going into the planning workshop, because in our experience it costs roughly 10 times more to make major changes in the design phase and 100 times more once the website is being built.

Ensure *all* of your key people are in the room. The start of the project is when everyone is most excited and least distracted. This is the opportunity to bring vision to the table and encourage ideas from all the different perspectives within your business.

While it may seem like overkill, you cannot overestimate the value of having everyone's buy-in and understanding of the project. There may be times when some people are not so involved, but this early participation is still not time wasted. On occasion we have cut corners and left people out of the loop because it seemed easier at the time…this is a major mistake and one that can lead to confused stakeholders, delayed signoffs, rework and budget blowouts.

So get everyone in the room upfront!

Pro Tip: Beware the 'Hippo'.

It is extremely important to get the **Hi**ghest **P**aid **P**erson's **O**pinion at the very beginning of the project, because if that person comes in late with new ideas, this can become the cause of project delays.

Table 6.1 outlines possible meeting participants. The list will depend on the size of your business; each role may be in-house or outsourced, and one person may have multiple responsibilities.

Table 6.1: suggested roles of the planning workshop participants

Role	Purpose for attendance
Business owner/CEO	To ensure alignment with strategic *business goals*
Marketing manager and marketing team	To ensure alignment with strategic *marketing goals*
CIO and technical team	To ensure alignment of strategic *technical requirements*
Designer	To ensure design consistency and understand *creative direction*
Frontline staff	To provide insights into common *questions and issues* they handle (for example, reception, sales)
Web developer	To understand the website *technical requirements*

The website blueprint

Knowing the broad goals of your strategy, it's time to nail down the details of your project. Just as when building a house, the time invested in creating a blueprint will make the designers' and the builders' jobs easier and ensure the accurate execution of the plan.

The four main components you'll need to define are:

1 content map

2 creative brief

3 wireframes

4 technical specifications.

We'll go into each of these in the following pages.

Pain #2: The content bottleneck

Another classic bottleneck for website projects is *content creation*. Generating the content and getting it signed off has often been a major roadblock for our clients—and for us.

On examination, we identified three elements that were causing the problem:

- Not *understanding* exactly what was needed for each page meant the creation process was ambiguous and often grossly underestimated.

- Not allocating *responsibility* for each piece of content meant that it was not produced.

- When Word documents bounced between multiple parties, content *version issues* could be appalling.

The solution came in two parts.

Content map

The first is the content map itself, which, when used alongside the wireframes gives a very detailed picture of exactly what will appear on each page.

A content map covers the following:

1 Your navigation aids:
   - main menu
   - submenus
   - footer menu
   - header menu
   - any other navigation tools

2   Mandatory items (such as licence numbers to be displayed, legal disclaimers, and terms and conditions)

3   Links appearing on each page

4   Outline of what is required on each page:
- images (photos, logos and so on)
- text
- videos
- links
- forms
- calls-to-action (such as 'Buy Now' buttons)
- other elements (maps, contact details and so on)

5   Dynamic elements, such as:
- associated blog posts
- related links
- related videos

Using this guide meant that everyone involved in the project knew exactly what content was to be created for each page — the ambiguity was gone.

Website content collaboration

'It worked, it worked!'

'What worked?'

'The Website Content Collaboration spreadsheet!'

'The content what?' Toby asked. 'Back it up, Lesley... What's this you're talking about?'

Content has been an enormous bottleneck for nearly every one of our projects. Particularly website projects.

In a previous life Toby would have paid significant sums of money *not* to have to reconcile one 40-page Word document full of edited content with another 40-page document containing *a different set of edits*. Perhaps you have mastered it (well done if you have!), but to him Word is simply not designed to cater for extensive collaboration between multiple parties. And organising your documents by the date on an email is a fundamentally flawed version control system.

'We managed to get all the content outlined, keyword focused, drafted, approved and uploaded on time. And we finished the project on the day we said we would.'

If you've been through a major rewrite of copy, then you know and understand the heartache and effort involved, and the enormous amount of time commonly lost to reworking and reviewing different versions.

So we put to work Lesley's native genius for taking ideas and making them actionable. She had created the Website Content Collaboration Template, which included:

- every piece of content
- who was responsible for writing it
- the keywords it was to focus on
- the associated images and videos
- the drafting and approval process.

It made an enormous difference.

This template enabled us to ensure the correct content was being created and approved by the right people, and helped us with version control—now we would always know which was the correct and current version.

Here are a few sample elements from our template:

1 page name

2 page title

3 focus keyword

4 hero image (the focus image for the page)

5 hero quote

6 sidebar image

7 sidebar quote

8 metadata (for your own use, invisible to visitors):
    - page title (70 characters)
    - page description (155 characters).

These elements are covered for each of the pages in the content map, each of which then has an approval process built into the Collaboration Template.

You can download the Website Content Collaboration Template from www.bluewiremedia.com.au/website-content-collaboration-template.

Using the template in tandem with the content map, we were able to keep the content process on track *and* up to date. It had an enormous impact on content delays.

Pain #3: Design disasters

The following are typical client problems we have fielded over the years:

- How do I get that 'wow' factor?

- My design looks out of date.

- It doesn't look consistent.

- How do I know it's working?

- How does design help our calls-to-action?

- Should we use stock images or real people?

- What information does a designer need?

One reason people get fed up with their own design is that as a business you spend a lot of time looking at it—*far more* time than any of your customers do.

But design is for your customer, not you.

Design decisions, like technology decisions or any other business decisions, should be based on what is going to get you the best *results*.

If you look at some of the most successful sites on the web, like Amazon or Google, what do you notice about their design? What do they have in common? Can you spot the 'wow' factor?

What you'll find is that they all have exceptional clarity of purpose and make it overwhelmingly easy to take action. At no point are you left wondering where you should go or what you should do next. As Steve Krug, usability expert and author of *Don't Make Me Think*, says, 'great design is invisible'. If your visitor has to think about what to do next, then you have raised a barrier to achieving the result you want.

> ## Pro Tip: Reduce the number of clicks.
>
> Have you noticed Amazon's 'Buy now with 1-Click®' button? Amazon eliminated clicks because it had noted the huge drop-off in conversions when you place a barrier (a click) in front of a prospective buyer. In our experience, the drop off is about 80 per cent per click. If you consider email, open rates are 20 per cent, and click-through rates are 20 per cent of that, so eight out of 10 people are dropping off at each click point.

What does a designer need to know?

Your designer needs to understand the strategic goals of your business and your customers' problems. This will dramatically influence the success of the design and therefore the overall project.

When briefing designers, make it clear that their design must help guide your customers along their path through your website.

Stock images vs your own photos

Stock images are easy—but they leave an impression of fakeness.

The reality is that we know intuitively when a photo is staged, rather than being of a real person associated with the business. When you don't use your own people or your own products in your photos, your authenticity is thrown into question.

Mobile

Very soon the internet will pass a crucial inflection point, when people will be accessing the web via mobile devices such as smartphones and tablets, more than by desktops. This needs to be a crucial consideration when setting up your website and infrastructure.

You need to consider mobile first *in your web design and in the way you structure your information.*

Users who visit your website via mobile might be looking for directions or trying to call you. It is likely they will be 'on the go' so making it really easy for them to find the information they need is your first priority.

The secret to designing for mobile is prioritising the pieces of content on each web page. Then you simply order them vertically in that priority for the mobile device. When we went through this process, we reduced the menu items down to three and decided that the top three priorities would be our home page, blog articles and calling us.

Creative brief

Because this is the visual component of the project, there are often plenty of people who want to weigh in. Make sure your web designer is present to capture the details of everyone's contributions to the vision for the project.

In our creative briefs, we use the following list to ensure we cover everything needed for a great design and look-and-feel. Most designers employ something similar, but you can use this as a guide for your project:

1 What are your key marketing messages?

2 What are good and poor features of your competitors' sites?

3 Which website is the creative benchmark you want to beat?

4 What are the key design considerations?
   - usability and user experience
   - look-and-feel
   - fonts.

5 Can you collect a series of images that would help you convey the look-and-feel you want to create?

6 What are the key content considerations?
   - tone of voice
   - style of photos and videos you'd like to use.

7 How will you use your credibility indicators and the proof of your remarkability?

8 What wireframes are required for the website? (We'll explain these next.)

Introducing wireframes

One part of the website-build process we had to rework constantly was the design. We needed to present multiple options—and frequently had to engage in major rework to get them right. Time and time again the journey from creative brief to design ran into a bottleneck.

Steve Krug introduced us to the concept of wireframes.

What are wireframes?

We define wireframes as black-and-white sketch drawings of the layout of your website. When working on the creative brief, we decide which pages are going to be different from one another. Typically the home page and multiple back pages need to be wireframed.

Sometimes we use Photoshop. At other times we use hand-drawn sketches in a notepad. The accuracy of the wireframe is less important than laying out all the elements so you can see how they will fit together on your site, to make it easy for your visitors to find what they need.

Make sure you wireframe the mobile version of your website too.

What are the results?

Since we began including wireframing as a mandatory step in our design process four years ago, we have had to undertake major redesign on *only one project*. This step on its own has saved us months of potential delays and rework across all of our projects.

Why do wireframes work?

Wireframes work because they separate layout decisions (such as where buttons are placed on a page) from visual design decisions (like the colour of the button). They begin the visual process *without the overwhelm*. There is no doubt they are incredibly effective in speeding up design and reducing rework.

Once the layouts are finalised, the colours and imagery can be crafted to complete the final visual design.

Pain #4: The build goes over time and over budget

Imagining new and wonderful ideas is easy when your minds are awash with all the possibilities of a new website. It's great to be excited about the project, but once you've agreed on the path during the initial planning, new ideas distract from the job at hand. What's most important is to stay focused on your plan.

Beware of feature creep.

Anyone who works in a software or creative role will tell you nearly anything is 'possible'. However, ditching the last good idea halfway through executing it to chase your new great idea is a fool's paradise. Keep all your new ideas in a list somewhere, and revisit it once your primary project is complete.

Pro Tip: Get the idea person to do the work.

Jason Fried from 37signals has a handy way of addressing the 'new idea' problem. He asks whoever comes up with the great idea to actually plan it and deliver it. Ideas aren't as much fun when they actually become 'work' so this simple strategy means only the ideas people feel most passionately about actually rise the to surface. It's a simple quality control measure, as well as a way to minimise feature creep on your own projects.

Technology decisions

The technology decision you make is very important. You need to understand your business and marketing strategy and your criteria for the final decision *before* you make it.

We've witnessed situations where technology decisions came first, costing companies literally hundreds of thousands of dollars in additional development, months in project delays, burned relationships and a huge emotional drain.

To avoid this mistake, nail down your strategy, content and functionality and then ask: What are the best technology options available to us to achieve our results?

Technical specification

Here are the elements we define in our website technical specification:

1 *Forms.* Define the field name, type, validation and whether it is mandatory for every form you require. Remember to include your anti-spam mechanisms (for example, Honey Pot Anti-Spam).

2 *Content management system.* Choose the one that best suits your content creators' needs and security and technology requirements. We commonly use WordPress because of its ease of use and abundant options for plug-ins, and because it has a huge development community for ongoing support.

3 *Editing capabilities.* Which areas of your website will you actually want to edit? Make sure these are listed in the technical specification.

4 *Content types and fields.* By defining content types and fields, you'll be able to control the consistency of styles across all of your content.

5 *Functionality and integrations.* This is where we might include elements to be integrated, such as blogs, email marketing software, Customer Relationship Management tools and so on.

6 *Testing and cross-browser compatibility.* Test for the current and recent versions of these browsers:
   - Internet Explorer
   - Firefox
   - Google Chrome
   - Safari
   - any others that are relevant to you.

7 *Mobile and apps.* Decisions need to be made on whether you require specialised apps, a mobile-specific site, or a responsive design. Each option has pros and cons; ask your web designer which is best for your business.

8 *Domains, hosting, emails.* It is a good idea to list all the domains you have registered and where they are hosted. This makes life easier for your web team. If your new site has specific hosting requirements, make sure they are included too.

9 *Ongoing maintenance.* Make sure there is a clear understanding on ongoing maintenance—it may mean simply getting help as required, or it may entail a more regular program.

Pain #5: Failure to communicate

We walked out of the client office, ordered a beer and sat down at a bar nearby. We were exhausted and exhilarated. We had just completed the biggest website project in Bluewire Media's history. Based on previous experience, it was a project that should have taken six months to complete. We'd done it in just four weeks.

In any project there will be elements you cannot foresee. After our horrendous experience of taking two years to complete a project, we realised that one huge issue with building websites is *communication* — particularly feedback and approval. This includes time spent waiting for feedback/ changes to come back to you as the other person works on it, or runs around the office getting approvals. Making changes to design and layout based on email feedback is extremely challenging. A phone call is a bit better. Face to face is the bomb.

So we borrowed again.

Synchronous communication

Verne Harnish, author of *Mastering the Rockefeller Habits* and CEO of Gazelles, shares his weekly newsletter with over 47 000 CEOs and business owners. We read it religiously.

One day he wrote about the difference between communication that is *synchronous* (when you get an immediate response, such as in a face-to-face meeting) as opposed to *asynchronous* (when you have to wait for the response, such as playing phone or email tag). He gave an example of how a business had used synchronous communication to win a huge contract with Boeing.

They had flown key members of their sales and engineering team from India to the US, and hired a hotel down the road from Boeing's headquarters. This was all so they could be close by and available for face-to-face questions throughout the tendering process, rather than going back and forth on email, telephone and video-conferencing hook-ups.

This example started us wondering if face-to-face might work in a project context too. And if so, how could we get to that point?

The next realisation emerged from a discussion with Dave Gardiner, Managing Director of Portland Group, who mentioned that nearly all of his projects ran on the client sites.

Armed with laptops, wireless, and cloud-based project management tools like Basecamp, we had everything we needed to work on site with the client.

Before arriving on site, here's how we set expectations with the client in our proposals:

Mutual expectations

Our commitment to you:

- We will remain on site until the project is complete.

- All deadlines are guaranteed.

- We will communicate in a timely, specific, appropriate and understandable manner.

- We will stick to the communication schedule.

- Issues will be discussed immediately as they arise.

Your commitment to us:

- You will provide direct access to *decision makers* for the duration of the project.

- You will stick to the agreed communication schedule.

- An appropriate, professional work area and internet access will be provided for the duration of the project.

- You will provide access to business premises during agreed working hours.

- All deadlines and responsibilities will be strictly met.

- All required information will be delivered on time.

- All task requests/revisions/changes, written approvals, events and important dates and file transfers will be handled via Bluewire Media's project management system (Basecamp).

- Issues will be discussed immediately as they arise.

Communication schedule

The final piece of the puzzle was creating a communication schedule with the client while we were on site. All of the approval points were prescheduled and booked into decision makers' diaries. It also meant booking in twice-daily 10-minute stand-up meetings at 10 am and 4 pm to go through the priorities and potential bottlenecks for the next half day.

You can download the Communication Schedule Template from www. bluewiremedia.com.au/communication-schedule-template.

Why working on site works

Here are some of the advantages of working on site:

1   *Focus.* Concentrating on one project at a time has incredible benefits that have been written about at length in other books.

2   *Energy.* When those involved see your project making progress, their energy lifts and feeds on itself to drive more.

3   *Accountability.* Working together transparently with your contracted web team means you know they are working on your project.

4   *Fast feedback.* Working on site means you have the benefit of *quick feedback on small things* that could cost you dearly in the long run. Having access to decision makers for the duration of the project is essential. Also, the feedback is much more accurate when colours can be tweaked, font sizes changed and elements moved around a screen in front of you.

5   *Synchronous communication.* This allows for the reading of body language (70 per cent of our communication), rather than just words or tone of voice, which make up the rest of our communication. Having twice-daily meetings also means you catch errors early, and at worst it affects half a day's work, not half a week's or half a month's—such a powerful difference.

These five key benefits of working on site will have an enormous impact on the speed and quality of your project.

Note: We realise that having everyone in the same room is not always possible. We've used Skype and Google Hangouts to facilitate synchronous communication and found that these work nearly as well.

Why speed matters

Here are three reasons why speed matters:

1   As Scott Belsky, author of *Making Ideas Happen*, points out, faster projects are much more energetic and rewarding.

2   Every project delay disproportionately increases the likelihood of further delays. Nassim Nicholas Taleb describes this phenomenon in his book *The Black Swan*.

3   Delays and overruns have a hidden cost. Every day, week or month that your website isn't up and working for you has a huge cost in forfeited leads and lost revenue.

Summary

For the fastest and best-quality web project you've ever undertaken, we suggest you follow these three steps:

→ Thrash upfront with everyone you need in the same room, at the same time.

→ Define your project well.

→ Work on site.

Tools and templates

Website Content Collaboration Template
www.bluewiremedia.com.au/website-content-collaboration-template

Web Design Checklist for Graphic Designers
www.bluewiremedia.com.au/website-checklist-for-graphic-designers

Communication Schedule Template
www.bluewiremedia.com.au/communication-schedule-template

Basecamp Project Management Tool
www.basecamp.com

Honey Pot Spam protection
www.projecthoneypot.org

99designs
www.99designs.com

Mastering the Rockefeller Habits by Verne Harnish

Don't Make Me Think by Steve Krug

The Black Swan by Nassim Nicholas Taleb

Making Ideas Happen by Scott Belsky

Chapter 7

Landing pages: design, psychology and leads

It's simple until we make it complicated.

Jason Fried

When we first co-created the Web Strategy Planning Template with David Meerman Scott in 2010, we decided to make it available on our website as a free download, no registration required. Using Google Analytics, we identified that the download rate was about 50 per cent, which was exciting. One in every two visitors to the page downloaded the template, and if they were passing it on to their friends and sharing it on social media, then our flagship content was being spread far and wide.

Nurturing your leads

That 50 per cent download rate was thrilling. On the downside, though:

- we didn't know who these people were
- we couldn't track whether or not they eventually became customers
- we had no way to connect with them
- we had no opportunity to deliver them more tools they might find useful.

These were pretty major flaws. So we decided to test it out by putting the template behind a simple form in which we asked for name and email address. The result? A conversion rate of 30 per cent, give or take, which at the time meant 30 people per week were signing up to download the template.

So it was a decent drop-off from a 50 per cent conversion rate, but the advantage was we knew who they were and could communicate with them and get to know them. As a marketer this is exactly what you want. Every single week we were getting 30-odd new leads coming to our business. For us, this was well worth 'missing out' on the other 20 per cent who weren't converting.

Of course, it's worth noting that not of all of these leads were 'sales ready', but they were interested in learning more. We had the opportunity to nurture this community with useful tools, articles and events.

Looking back at the clients we've won in the past 12 months, nearly all of our customers and clients have downloaded this tool during their information-gathering phase. In fact, our highest paying clients have told us that the intellectual capital contained in the template was the key reason they decide to engage our firm.

Without doubt, landing pages are crucial, second only to your flagship content as the secret sauce of web marketing. They work in tandem to deliver you knockout results. Your flagship content without a landing page is like having great conversations with prospects but forgetting to exchange business cards and never getting their names. A lost opportunity.

Landing pages are the most overlooked ingredient in the web marketing system.

What is a landing page?

A landing page is purpose-built to generate leads on your website. Visitors can download a piece of your premium content, such as an e-book, template, report, calendar or PDF in exchange for their details. When they do so, this is called a *conversion*.

As content marketers, one of our main objectives is to build our audience and attract new leads, and landing pages facilitate this perfectly. They allow a visitor to enter a name and email address in exchange for access to a premium piece of content. The benefit is that you grow your email list, and, at the same time, the visitor gets to learn how to solve a problem. Your organisation is helping prospects, sharing its smarts with the world and being seen as a thought leader.

Two approaches to growing your community

One of Australia's most prolific and widely read bloggers, Jeff Bullas, has said publicly that his biggest regret was not putting an email signup form on his website sooner.

Jeff had planned to fix his email sign up form in 2011 but stalled. When he finally did so in 2013, it was soon attracting over 100 conversations a day. He estimates his inaction had cost him 72 800 subscribers, but fortunately his enormous blog following meant he could amass a huge email base in a short amount of time. Keep in mind that email subscribers are one of the closest relationships you can attract online.

On the other hand, David Meerman Scott advocates giving away your content completely free, without email registration, because his personal experience is that your ideas will travel as much as 50 times further that way.

When we compared the two approaches, we preferred having our content behind a registration form, since the drop-off in downloads was significantly outweighed by the earnings from paying clients.

Failure to implement landing pages may mean the growth of your email list will stall, and you could be tempted to give up. When you do get your landing pages set up, you'll get that 'marketer's rush' whenever someone downloads your content and your community grows. You're not only helping them but gaining more leads *with no additional effort.*

Aside from the obvious commercial benefits, there is a genuine sense of reward that comes from the fact that you've actually helped someone solve a problem at the moment they've needed it. In doing so you're contributing to the greater community.

That's web marketing that works.

Anatomy of a successful landing page

Landing pages come in all shapes and sizes, and are subject to incredible scrutiny and testing. As always, test what works for you, but the following basics are most effective. Our own testing at Bluewire supports this. By industry standards, an overall website conversion rate of 2 to 3 per cent is considered high. Since implementing landing pages for ourselves, our overall website conversion rate of 6 to 8 per cent has remained consistent for years. That's two to three times what is considered 'high'. We were proud to attract 5617 leads via these landing pages in 2012 and receive an international award for it (as discussed on p. 45).

Landing page basics

According to the e-book *The Ultimate Guide to Conversion Centered Design* by Oli Gardner, you need to include the following elements on your landing pages: in the *design*, encapsulation, contrast and colour, directional cues and white space; in the *psychology*, urgency and scarcity, try before you buy and social proof. Figure 7.1 is a screenshot of one of Bluewire Media's landing pages so you can see these principles in action:

- *Encapsulation.* The form has a blue border that 'encapsulates' it.

- *Contrast and colour.* The orange call-to-action button stands out from and contrasts with the blue of the form.

- *Directional cues.* The headshot of Jonathan faces towards the form and there are two arrows—all of which give directional cues to guide the user to the form.

- *White space.* The page is open and uncluttered, with enough space for the user's eyes to focus comfortably on the form.

- *Urgency and scarcity.* Typically this doesn't apply to lead-generation landing pages because nothing is for sale. However, on sales pages it is common. For example, airline websites might say: 'Hurry, only 5 seats left!'

- *Try before you buy.* You can preview the template via an embedded Slideshare file.

- *Social proof.* The social media share numbers give us proof that other people have liked, tweeted, +1'd and shared the template. We also include the message 'Join 10,512 other savvy marketers', indicating the number of visitors—there's safety in numbers.

Figure 7.1: Bluewire Media landing page

Download the Landing Page Design Template from www.bluewiremedia .com.au/landing-page-design-template.

Remove leaks

Leaks in a boat's hull are bad news. A landing page also needs to avoid leaks—links that allow visitors to click away from the page to other websites, social media or even other pages on your website. By simply removing all links, you are making it easier for the visitor to stay focused on the job they came to do.

Remove navigation menu

The biggest win is removing your main navigation. The objective is to help visitors to complete the task at hand without getting distracted and clicking through to a different section, clicking out of your site, or doing something else away from their computer, laptop or device. Don't worry, you can give them all your website options *after* they've filled in the form.

Eliminate distractions

Make sure it is super-clear what you want the visitor to do once they get to your landing page. Never underestimate the power of simplicity and clear calls-to-action. *No one* (other than you, maybe) will ever be 100 per cent focused on your landing page, so you've got to make it easy.

People who find your landing page will be on a phone or tablet, on the train or bus or in the airport lounge, or perhaps on a work computer with 20 other open tabs all vying for their attention, or maybe at home on the laptop, cooking dinner and watching TV at the same time. So unless you make it extraordinarily easy, you'll miss your chance.

Eliminate options

For lead-generation landing pages, you want to give the visitors only *one decision to make*: to download or not to download. If you introduce other options, suddenly they need to *think*, to weigh them up. This can become too hard very quickly, so they abandon the landing page. *Option overwhelm* is known to lower conversion rates significantly, and the more options you offer the more it will undermine your efforts. However, it's worth noting that on sales landing pages, providing a few pricing options can be very effective — but different principles are at play.

Pro Tip: Maximise your thank you page.

If you want to introduce a second offer, do it after the form is completed. For example, on the thank you page or in the thank you email, add 'You may also be interested in our second offer...'

Our Web Strategy Planning Template landing page is purpose-built to convert. It follows all of the principles we've outlined and converts at a rate of over 30 per cent. Compare that to our home page, where we include a call-to-action to download the Web Strategy Planning Template, but where visitors will also find our main navigation and other leaks. This page converts at only 2 per cent.

There's a big difference in the intent of people who land on our home page, who may be there for any number of reasons. Of course you need your navigation and other content on your home page, but it highlights how much distractions and leaks decrease the conversion rate. Nevertheless, the home page is usually the most trafficked page of a website, and the more conversions you can land from it the better, so ...

Put your flagship content on your home page too.

> ## Pro Tip: Add your flagship content as a pop-up.
>
> Some people find pop-ups annoying, but testing shows they are highly effective and have a negligible impact on the bounce rate. You can set the offer to appear after, say, 15 or 30 seconds, once the visitor has had a chance to read some of the post. Try WordPress's WP Popup Plugin.

Keep your form simple

Filling out forms that ask for unnecessary information is a cause of friction and leads to people abandoning your page.

Only ask for information that is relevant and that you intend to use.

You will have plenty of time to collect more information about the person in future so, for the landing page, the shorter your form, the better your conversion rate will be.

Make the offer compelling

This applies equally to your flagship content and your landing page. In the words of Jay Baer, the quality should be so great that people would be happy to *pay* for it.

Remember, if visitors need to enter an email address to download the resource, they know they are likely to receive further emails from your organisation. Everyone's been burned by spam, so why should they see you as different? Tell them if you are going to send more emails, and what they can expect to gain by opening them. Ours clearly states:

> You'll also receive the weekly Bluewire News, free templates and event invites.

Visitors need to feel a high level of confidence that you are trustworthy. Why should they trust you with their email address?

Provide a preview of the download

The best way to make your offer compelling is to let your visitors sample the goods first. For digital content like e-books and templates, we suggest uploading them to Slideshare and embedding a preview of the resource on your landing page. This has been effective for Bluewire Media's landing pages because visitors can flick through the pages of an e-book, and even read the entire e-book on the full-screen version. They can then be very confident of why they are trading their email address.

Before you ask, yes, of course they could go straight to Slideshare and download it with no email registration, and people do. That's fine by us. Just as people forward templates and e-books to friends, it's very flattering that people are interested in our content. If they like it, perhaps they will come back for one of our other free tools and register with their email then.

Some marketers have a different view here, but with an overall website conversion rate of 6 to 8 per cent, ours does better than most company websites we have come across. The only major difference is that we let visitors preview what they are getting. Give it a go, and see if it works for you.

More social proof

People crave security. We love the assurance that other people have tried something out and given it the thumbs-up. Include Twitter, Facebook, LinkedIn and +1 buttons so people can share the page, and so you can demonstrate that other people endorse it too. Testimonials also achieve this.

Another effective piece of social proof is to mention how many other people are in your community already. For example, the following marketing experts all recognise this power:

- Joe Pulizzi (Content Marketing Institute): 'Join over 70 000 of your peers'

- Ann Handley (MarketingProfs): 'Join 626 000 marketing professionals'

- Jay Baer (Convince and Convert): 'Join 21 000 of your peers'

- Leo Widrich (Buffer App): 'Join 10 629 other good-looking people who get free email updates'.

Get traffic direct to your landing page

The usual conversion tip is to put your flagship content on your blog sidebar and as a pop-up. This is sound advice, but since blog readers are relatively passive, it's much harder to steer people to convert. Whereas people who arrive at your distraction-free landing page (especially from Google) are typically seeking specific content and are ready to take action.

Your blog is an important part of your marketing system, but not the best place to start.

How to optimise for search

We take the time to do some keyword research using Google Instant and Übersuggest to find popular phrases that have reasonable search volume. We'll cover search optimisation in greater detail in chapter 12.

Pro Tip: Optimise your landing pages for search.

A secret tactic that we've employed is to give your landing page a name that matches what people are Googling. Then, when you get some good-quality backlinks to it, it will appear in Google results when people search for it. This puts lead generation on autopilot and minimal extra work is required once you've set it up. Every month more than 500 new people opt in via one of our landing pages, nearly a third via search engines. Even when we don't blog, tweet or take any other action, and even while we're on holiday, we still get hundreds of new leads.

After we named the Web Strategy Planning Template and set up the landing page, we discovered that the phrase 'digital strategy template' also had a high search volume. Knowing this, we simply optimised the page for this phrase too. Specifically, we added those exact words to the landing page's title, as a subheading, in the intro text and in the page copy. We now get traffic and leads from people searching for 'digital strategy template' too. Little tweaks like this can yield big results.

Web marketing is a work in progress that you can continuously improve.

> ### Pro Tip: Use Google authorship so your headshot shows in search results.
>
> When Rand Fishkin from Moz gave his keynote at Inbound12, he explained that when your headshot appears in search results, you'll get more clicks, often even more than the top results. We implemented this technique immediately and saw a 13 per cent increase in leads for that month. *Simple tweaks, big results.*
>
> The best how-to article we've found on this is at http://blog.kissmetrics.com/google-authorship.

Buttons

Call-to-action buttons and the words you use have an important, sometimes underestimated impact on conversion. Here are some key considerations:

- *Use active words on the button.* Think carefully about the words you use as your call-to-action on the button. They need to describe the action very clearly. Some effective ones are: 'Free Instant Access', 'Download Template' and 'Access My e-Book'.

- *The best calls-to-action are verb–noun.* But don't be afraid to use buttons with quite a few words.

- *Think about what the user wants.* A very easy way to decide what words to use on the button is to finish this sentence for the user: 'I want to ...'—for example, '... download the 33-page e-book' or '... watch the video interview right now'.

A word of warning: avoid the word *submit*. You submit taxes and exam assignments, neither of which is usually fun ... Leave submit for the taxman and the schoolteacher.

> ### Pro Tip: Use the word *template.*
>
> Our three best-performing landing pages are our Web Strategy Planning Template, Editorial Calendar Template and Social Media Guidelines Template, which contribute more than 70 per cent of our conversions.

Summary

→ Landing pages are as important to your website as your business cards are at an event.

→ Landing pages are the perfect way to exchange your flagship content for someone's name and email address.

→ Remove leaks like the main navigation and provide just one option so it's simple to take action.

→ Only ask for information that you absolutely need.

→ Use design components such as encapsulation, directional cues and colour-contrasting download buttons.

→ Provide social proof that your content is worth downloading.

Tools and templates

Social Media Planning Template
www.bluewiremedia.com.au/social-media-planning-template

Social Media Guidelines Template
www.bluewiremedia.com.au/free-social-media-guidelines-template

Editorial Calendar Template
www.bluewiremedia.com.au/editorial-calendar-template

Landing Page Design Template
www.bluewiremedia.com.au/landing-page-design-template

Übersuggest
www.ubersuggest.com

Google Instant
www.google.com/instant

Google Keyword Planner
https://adwords.google.com/keywordtool

Slideshare
www.slideshare.com

'How to Set Up Google Authorship'
http://blog.kissmetrics.com/google-authorship/

The Ultimate Guide to Conversion Centered Design e-book by Oli Gardner
http://get.unbounce.com/conversion-centered-design-guide/

'How procrastination cost me 72,800 email subscribers'
www.jeffbullas.com/2013/08/08/how-procrastination-cost-me
-72800-email-subscribers/

Part IV

Content creation

Chapter 8

Email marketing: the ultimate tool for web marketers

When you serve others, you'll grow. It really is that simple.

Michael Stelzner

Numerous web marketing folk have told us: 'You live and die by your database'. The term *database* doesn't do it justice, of course; we're talking about a community of people with whom you have a relationship. That is, people who know, like and trust you enough to have given permission to receive your updates in their inbox. The money lies in the quality of the relationships, not the size of the list, which is why buying lists is such a monumental waste of time, money and reputation.

My database is worth nothing in your hands, and vice versa.

We completely agree with Chris Brogan on the relative value of one email subscriber against 20+ Twitter followers. Fortunately for us, social media didn't exist when we started out, so email was the only way to grow an audience of subscribers. Social media is sexy and gets all the headlines these days, but we actually consider email the original form of 'social media' because it can be one-to-one or one-to-many, it can go viral, and it is very social.

Everyone uses email

The pillar of our web marketing has been the strength of our network, and email is the best electronic way to keep our network strong. Networks require nourishment, pruning and harvesting, and we'll show you how. Email marketing remains, as much as ever, the ultimate tool in the web marketer's arsenal.

In fact, if given the choice of a social media platform such as Facebook, Twitter or LinkedIn, or email as a marketing instrument, we'd take email every time. LinkedIn is making a strong surge, but while social media complements email, we're convinced that email should remain your primary focus. You can start the relationship with people on social media but then you should focus on nurturing until they trust you with their email address.

In terms of sales, email remains the best online conversion tactic.

In relation to one of his product launches, Chris Brogan noted that social media accounted for only 10 per cent of sales, with the remaining 90 per cent coming from email. If you compound that with the fact that his social media following was actually 10 times bigger than his email list, you can argue from these results that email punches 100 times above social media when it comes to sales. This reflects our experiences with our own events, online courses and products.

Why email over social media?

There are a number of reasons, but the principal one is that nearly everyone is on email, while not everyone is active on social media. Email stays in an inbox until it's read (though it can be ignored or deleted), but you must be logged in to your social media streams to see the content—otherwise you miss it. Most professionals sit with their email open all day long. To do so with social media is typically frowned on.

But who wants more email?

In keynote presentations, Adam often asks who'd like more email? Few hands go up. (Unless it's PayPal notifying you that money has landed in your account—those messages are always welcome!) Even fewer admit to *wanting* unsolicited email from strangers. This presents marketers with a challenge but also an opportunity. The challenge is enticing people to sign up and stay signed up; the opportunity is to deliver emails that are truly anticipated and valued.

We always open emails from friends

When faced with an overflowing inbox, whose emails do we click on first? Emails from friends and people we like, of course! As email marketers our goal should be to deliver emails that are as personal, friendly and as useful as emails sent from friends.

First lesson learned

During our first year in business, Adam kicked off the first Bluewire News email. We spent our first six months growing our database of friends, family and business contacts, which amounted to just over 700 people.

We'd written, designed and developed the very first Bluewire News and tested the email to make sure it looked fine in the inboxes of different 'email clients' (in marketing jargon) such as Hotmail, Outlook, Yahoo and Gmail. Everything was double, triple and quadruple checked and it all seemed A-OK, but Adam was a nervous wreck. Not only were we in business for the first time, but we were telling everyone we knew what we'd been up to. A very confronting experience but one we felt we needed to get used to.

So he took a deep breath and hit Send, then waited for it to arrive in his inbox, and it duly did—addressed to 'Dear Adam'. The penny dropped: He'd sent 'Dear Adam' to the entire database! This was okay for the three people on the database called Adam, but not so cool for everyone else. Adam's stomach dropped, but he had to get himself together. He'd messed up and needed to fix the situation.

He decided to admit his mistake immediately and resend the email with 'Oops, sorry' in the subject line. The moral of this story is always get a second set of eyes to look over your emails, and also remember we are all human and that when mistakes inevitably happen it's best to be honest and act quickly and with humility.

Content people gravitate towards

In his book *Content Chemistry*, Andy Crestodina describes an experiment he ran on people waiting to enter one of his workshops.

On the table in the waiting area he had placed three items: a brochure, a magazine and a book. Andy wanted to see what type of content people gravitated to. It turns out that most people picked up the brochure and put it straight back down once they realised it was an ad; they picked up the book, looked at its cover and put it back down, but they picked up and started reading and flicking through the magazine. The same idea can be applied to email newsletters.

Let's take a look at what makes a successful email newsletter. Remember, the purpose of these communications is to deliver value to your readers, to humanise your business, and to allow you and your readers to get to know each other better.

It's people who know, like and trust you who become your customers.

Email type 1: regular email newsletters

The most common type of marketing email is your regular newsletter. Many companies send these emails and they vary widely in quality. At their worst they are typically full of ads and promotional offers, and very few of these would be missed. Unless—and it's a big caveat—that's what you signed up to receive, as with Daily Deals or Groupon. At the other end of the spectrum are the emails you look forward to receiving and you would miss if they didn't turn up in your inbox.

When Adam spoke with Dan Zarrella after his 'Science of Inbound Marketing' presentation at Inbound12, he said his experiments indicated that it was effective to email a lot more often than monthly. Dan argued that once a month is actually not frequent enough because people will tend to forget about you during that interval. He recommended at least weekly and cited examples of daily emails (news digests, for example) that had built solid readerships. Since 2013 was to be the year of marketing experiments, we decided to put this theory to work.

Marketing experiment 1: monthly vs weekly emails

With renewed vigour and science on our side, we started 2013 with an experiment in which we increased the frequency of Bluewire News from monthly to weekly. Our open rates went from averaging 25 per cent on the first send of our monthly newsletter, down to 19 per cent for our weekly newsletter. Click-through rates remained consistent.

Something that Seth Godin blogged was triggered in Adam's mind. Seth had decided 'to write for his existing readers, rather than writing to convert the masses'. Adam also preferred to write for engaged core readers rather than trying to persuade the uninterested or emotionally unsubscribed. We decided that interacting weekly with some 2000 engaged, regular readers was better than drawing an extra 500 readers but communicating only monthly.

Marketing experiment 2: text-only vs HTML emails

Two of the email newsletters we most look forward to are Verne Harnish's and Chris Brogan's. Both are text-only, and we know exactly when to expect them in our inbox each week. Chris gets a 61 per cent open rate on his 61 000 subscribers (although he doesn't include subscribers who haven't opened anything in the past six months), while Verne gets 20 per cent on his 47 000-strong list. This is how both Chris Brogan and Verne Harnish drive the bulk of their business.

Since our motto is to emulate the people we like best, we tested a text-only email that's just how it looks, as if sent via Gmail or Outlook, against our usual graphic-designed, HTML-style newsletter. For us, text-only emails worked best when the From Name was an individual, like 'Toby Jenkins' as opposed to the company 'Bluewire Media', and we'll explain how we use these for maximum effect a little later.

Marketing experiment 3: Sending a follow-up email

One day in 2010 we decided to test how many people who hadn't opened Bluewire News during that week opened a follow-up email on the weekend. All we changed was the subject line—to read 'Did you miss August's Bluewire News ...?' We were excited to see a 7 to 10 per cent open rate on the follow up. The unsubscribe rate stayed nice and low, well under 0.5 per cent, so we decided to do this every month. We now change the subject line of the weekend follow-up email to feature a different aspect of that week's Bluewire News. It consistently draws a 7 to 12 per cent open rate, which equates to about 900 readers per week.

Pro Tip: Make it personal – ask for replies.

Every Bluewire News post comes with a personal welcome from us, and usually an invitation to reply if they want to get in touch or if they have any questions. On its own, this doesn't usually solicit a huge response rate, but it does underscore that we are accessible.

The real game changer for us was when we gave readers an easy excuse to get in touch. In our case it was by answering a riddle or brain-teaser. It could quite easily be a trivia or multiple-choice question—anything informal that initiates a casual conversation. The result? Each week Adam's inbox is full of riddle replies—a fun, casual way to get to know our most interested readers.

Marketing experiment 4: content that gets clicked

We've tested and measured the click-through rates on all our email newsletters, and the results are quite conclusive.

1 Downloadable templates are, hands down, the best type of content, with a click-through rate of 26 to 66 per cent. Note that normally people are asked to type their details into the landing page form to access these downloads. But, since we already know them (because they receive our newsletter), we don't put them through these hoops to access the content. So no registration process is required for an instant download.

2 E-books have a click-through rate of 10 to 33 per cent.

3 The next most popular content is usually a featured blog post, with a click-through rate of 5 to 14 per cent.

4 Expert interviews score surprisingly low, with a click-through rate of 3 to 7 per cent. When repurposed into an e-book, however, these interviews have a much higher click-through rate. Perhaps people appreciate the convenience of having the content packaged in an e-book they can read later.

5 Riddles and brain-teasers don't technically have a click-through rate, but we measure the response rate based on readers who reply to the email with their answer. This is usually between 2 and 4 per cent.

For us, this opens the door for one-on-one conversations, where we can get to know our readers better! Riddles are a great conversation starter (much like chatting to people in real life), and they are more effective than jumping straight into a 'business conversation', which can typically make people uneasy because they fear they will be sold to or pressured into a meeting.

6 Finally, pictures are always a favourite in newsletters. We are social animals. Including pictures adds personality to your company, and readers simply like seeing what other people are up to!

Pro Tip: Make sure your email marketing is independent of your web team.

If you're anything like us, you'll find yourself compiling, sending and testing your newsletters whenever inspiration strikes. You don't want to be constantly interrupting your web team, as we were guilty of! They might be busy, or it could be after hours, and your inspiration will need to be put on hold until tomorrow.

Life was certainly a lot easier for all involved when Adam could do it all by himself. The team at Bluewire set up two email templates that were robust enough for a non-techie (Adam) to use and send, with no issues. The two we had were our Bluewire News template, which was in colour and included images (our HTML email), and the text-only template, which looked identical to an email we would send through Gmail—black text, white background and a regular email signature.

Pro Tip: Own a send time.

There's no right time of day to send, because very often you'll have readers in all time zones of the world. For the best results, pick a regular time to send and stick to it. Then your readers will know exactly when to expect your emails. For example, we know that Chris Brogan's email will arrive on Sunday night (Australian time) and Verne Harnish's will arrive Friday morning.

Email type 2: lead-nurturing autoresponder emails

You can set up lead-nurturing emails using autoresponders with most email marketing systems. It means you can drip-feed specific emails to people once they opt in. If someone downloads content from your landing page, you can send them an email with related content after a set time period, such as seven days.

We drip-feed our best templates every week and our lead-nurturing autoresponder series looks like this:

Email 1 (immediately): Welcome to Bluewire
Email 2 (after 7 days): [FREE TEMPLATES] Our 3 best marketing templates
Email 3 (after 14 days): [FREE TEMPLATES] Social media templates
Email 4 (after 21 days): [FREE TEMPLATES] Content marketing templates

Download your Lead Nurturing Template from www.bluewiremedia.com .au/lead-nurturing-template.

For us, both open rates and click-through rates exceed 40 per cent — double that of our Bluewire News emails. This is because a subscriber is getting our very best premium content at convenient intervals.

> ## Pro Tip: Send a birthday email.
>
> Sending readers a special email on their birthday will produce open rates that will blow your mind—expect well over 50 per cent, and a happy reader!

Email type 3: text only (your secret sales weapon)

Gmail-style (or Outlook-style, depending on your preference), text-only emails have no images, and for us they have an open rate as high as 35 per cent.

The personal touch

Emails sent from an individual's account that look like personal rather than marketing emails always perform better. Very occasionally someone may feel a bit misled by this because they thought your email was written only to them, so you need to consider what you feel comfortable with as a marketer. Our rule of thumb is to indicate that the email is marketing- or work-related by including Bluewire Media with the signature (Toby Jenkins—Bluewire Media) or in the subject line (Bluewire Event).

When we tested the performance of these text-only emails against the HTML versions of our regular Bluewire News, the difference in open rate was insignificant. In fact, a lot of the feedback was along the lines of: 'I prefer the usual design, it doesn't look as nice, and the design contributes a lot to the feel of the newsletter'.

One call-to-action, one sender

The best use of text-only emails has been in direct response emails, especially sales emails. Email is usually a forum for actually taking action when it comes to buying things. If you're committing to a new vendor, you'll receive the email from an individual and often you'll respond directly to it.

When you get to the point where you have a valuable offer for your readers and you're inviting them to check out a paid product, the best format we've tested is a text email from an individual. You can include text links that take people to the Buy Now page. We certainly found this to be the best approach. Newsletters are a great format for making people aware of what's coming up—such as events, e-books or toolkits—but when you want to convert readers into buyers, text is far more powerful.

> ### Pro Tip: Buck the trend.
>
> This technique works because it breaks the rhythm you've set with your regular newsletter emails. We consistently send Bluewire News emails as HTML from Bluewire Media at 6 am on Wednesday. Then we buck the trend and send a text email from Adam Franklin during business hours on a Monday and it really gets readers' attention.

For example, we included information about our web marketing workshop in three Bluewire News emails, then, three days out from the cutoff date for early bird tickets, Adam sent a text-only email from his personal email account and, as always, wrote it as if he was writing to *one* person, rather than to 9000.

Within the space of two days we'd sold $7000 worth of tickets, which went directly into our PayPal account. No invoices to issue, no follow-up payments—money in the bank!

In chapter 15, we'll delve further into selling online without losing your integrity.

Pruning your list

There comes a time in many relationships when it's best to move on, and email subscription relationships are no different. If we see in our reports that people haven't opened one of our emails in 6 to 12 months or more, we'll trigger a 'break-up email'.

Every 12 or 18 months we trawl through our reports to see who has not opened a single email in all that time. In those cases, we'll send out our break-up email, which goes like this:

From: Bluewire Media

Subject line: Is it time to go?

Hi James,

How are you?

It's been quite some time since you've opened one of our Bluewire News emails, so we just wanted to check that you still want to receive them. If you do, <u>please click here to confirm</u>.

However, there's no hard feelings if you unsubscribe, and if you don't respond we'll remove you from our list so we no longer bother you.

All the best,

Adam & Toby

More email marketing experiments

Here are some more results of email marketing experiments we've run.

'From Name' experiments

Adam Franklin and Toby Jenkins vs Bluewire Media

Bluewire Media won this test by 10 per cent. With our egos shattered, we tested it twice more and it won again—by 6 per cent and then by 31 per cent. In retrospect, it was understandable that more people would now be familiar with the company name rather than with its founders. In the early days, when we tested this out our personal names outperformed because our email subscribers were mainly friends, family and contacts we each knew personally.

Toby Jenkins vs Bluewire Media

Toby Jenkins won this convincingly by 34 per cent, which makes sense because it looks like it could be a personal message from Toby. Despite occasional reader resistance, most email subscribers know that emails you send will be part of a mass mail-out.

'Subject line' experiments

BLUEWIRE NEWS vs Bluewire News

The capitals won this A/B split test by 13 per cent. The capitals make the first part of the subject line pop out of an inbox, although running the entire subject line in capitals would be far too spam-like and risk making readers feel they were being yelled at.

[FREE E-BOOK] vs [E-BOOK]

The four-letter F word is always a controversial one. In our test [FREE E-BOOK] outperformed [E-BOOK] by 7 per cent.

[INVITE] LinkedIn Masterclass vs LinkedIn Masterclass

The first version won this test by 27 per cent.

Email body-copy experiment: long copy vs short copy

Short copy won by 100 per cent. When we launched our Web Marketing That Works online course, the short copy version of our email had twice as many click-throughs to the Buy Now page.

Summary

→ Email marketing is easily the most effective form of web marketing.

→ Keep building your email list and start communicating with your readers via a weekly newsletter.

→ Deliver value every time, and get to know your readers better.

→ Set up a lead-nurturing autoresponder series for new subscribers.

→ When it's time to invite readers to enter into a commercial relationship with your organisation, go with text-only emails.

Tools and templates

Lead Nurturing Template
www.bluewiremedia.com.au/lead-nurturing-template

Campaign Monitor
www.campaignmonitor.com

MailChimp
www.mailchimp.com

Vision 6
www.vision6.com.au

'7 Sales Secrets From My Best Sales Day Ever' by Chris Brogan
www.chrisbrogan.com/sales-secrets

Chapter 9

From blogging to content marketing: attracting leads, not just readers

Good artists copy; great artists steal.

Steve Jobs

Blogging has been a bittersweet experience for us. Too often we've heard it said that if you consistently publish great content on your blog, you'll magically attract traffic, social shares and inbound leads. The cream will rise to the top and all your marketing dreams will come true. To perpetuate this thinking would be irresponsible. It simply isn't true.

Many people fall off the blogging bandwagon because they are sold this dream, only to be faced with the hard reality of investing loads of effort but gaining zero traction. We've been there. We've flirted with the idea of giving up on blogging. Was it worth the time? When would we see results? Both pertinent questions that a business owner and web marketer must ask.

Why were we missing the mark?

Our own company blog has had the fortune of being named among Australia's Top 25 business blogs in every list that SmartCompany has put out since 2010. But in the early days there were times when we contemplated giving up.

Even now, despite the accolades, to assume that every post is a traffic magnet would be a huge mistake. We've had some big hits and some bigger misses. We've put in hours of work in writing, editing, linking and posting an article, only to get readers numbering in the single digits, with no comments, no shares and no backlinks. It can be demoralising.

Why were the experts still preaching that once you start blogging, all your marketing dreams would come true? The truth is that blogging is only half the story.

You need readers

As a blogger and content marketer, you need readers. Sounds too obvious to say, but we forget.

> ### Pro Tip: Syndicate your content.
>
> Give permission for other blogs to syndicate your content with attribution to get your content in front of new readers.

As we've mentioned, we follow the basic principle of emulating the people who do it best, and Jeff Bullas is one of Australia's (and the web's) most prolific bloggers. One day Adam stumbled across one of Jeff's articles on the Business2Community blog, along with the acknowledgement that it had been 'syndicated with permission'.

So he reached out to Jeff to check that he had in fact given permission, which he had. From there Adam figured there was no need to reinvent the wheel so he contacted the Business2Community team to find out what we needed to do to get our blog up there too. They looked over our blog and gave it the green light. From there it proved very simple to start getting our posts syndicated and posted on their blog.

What? 100 tweets?

Suddenly our content was planted in front a much bigger audience — bigger to the tune of over 500 000 readers per month. Not all of them read our posts, of course, but it is a much bigger pond to be playing in. Our jaw dropped when we first took a look at the social media shares. Over 100 tweets? Whoa! When you're used to 10 tweets in total, with seven of them coming from your colleagues, this was huge. Huge in terms of readership and huge for our confidence as bloggers.

It also demonstrated that all blog posts aren't created equal. If exactly the same piece of content got hardly any traction on Bluewire Media's blog but could explode on Business2Community, then *where* we put our content clearly mattered a lot.

Social proof

So if syndicating our content was so powerful, where else could we reach an existing audience? We now felt as though we had sufficient skill to 'cut it' in the blogging world. Our writing skill was unchanged, but the confidence boost that came with our newfound audience was enormous.

We instantly felt like better writers because the social proof was there.

Business2Community isn't the only high-traffic and reputable blog that syndicates blog content, but it is a great place to start if you blog about anything loosely related to business.

Aside from the new audience we get every time they syndicate a post, the unforeseen benefits have included having articles syndicated again to websites like Yahoo! Small Business, which has brought our content to even more readers.

Where else could we seed our content and piggyback on other existing audiences?

Guest blogging

In a stroke of good timing, Adam was invited to be a foundation guest blogger on the StartupSmart website, which was aimed at helping Australian entrepreneurs. It was certainly lucky that he caught the attention of the newly appointed editor, but Adam probably wouldn't have been so fortunate had he not had over 100 blog posts to his name and a body of work that showcased his writing.

Adam's fortnightly column on this website has been running since 2011. It's the place where many of our existing customers first found out about Bluewire, and where a huge number of our regular subscribers have come from.

Other unforeseen benefits have included having articles reposted on StartupSmart's sister site SmartCompany, which has a very strong and active readership.

> ## Pro Tip: Include a call-to-action.
>
> Always include in your blog a call-to-action linking to your flagship content landing page. It's particularly important to include your call-to-action in the body of your post so that when the article is syndicated, the backlink remains.

It is very exciting to write for someone else's audience, and a huge opportunity for web marketers. One of the most important things you can do is allow readers to pursue their relationship with you if they are keen to learn more. We see it as a duty to offer readers more content to delve into if they've enjoyed our guest blog post. The way to do this is to invite readers to click through to one of your landing pages, where of course you'll have a purpose-built page where people can register their name and email in exchange for your premium content.

For example, at the end of one of his StartupSmart posts Adam included the following call-to-action.

> To keep your marketing useful, it is handy to document your strategy in a one-page plan. To help you out, here's the Web Strategy Planning Template — it's a **free download**. ['free download' was linked]

You'll see it's relevant and is a gentle invitation aimed at interested readers. You can easily write calls-to-action that are non-aggressive and non-salesy.

Between StartupSmart and SmartCompany, where it was reposted, this content attracted more than 100 new leads in one day. And because it continues to be a popular article that readers stumble across on both websites, as well as on Google, this one guest blog post continues to deliver a trickle of new leads every month.

Every time Adam's guest articles get posted he can expect between 20 and 50 new leads. These leads are then nurtured with further emails, and go into our regular Bluewire News correspondence.

> **Pro Tip: Write more for other people than you do for your own blog.**
>
> Remember, even if your own blog currently has no one reading it, you can give your content an audience by reaching out to bloggers who might publish your writing. This is the secret tactic for growing your readership, growing backlinks to your blog and therefore increasing it's visibility.

Content Chemistry author Andy Crestodina writes 50 articles a year for other people's blogs versus 25 articles for his own blog. He aims to write for the big blogs once a year. Barry Feldman, a regular writer for Hubspot, Marketing Profs, Social Media Today, Convince and Convert and Copyblogger, produces most of his best work for other people, which has made him something of a content marketing celebrity in the blogging world.

> **Pro Tip: Aim for email subscribers over RSS subscribers.**
>
> Having RSS (Really Simple Syndication) subscribers is great—but to communicate with them you must write a blog post, whereas if you collect readers' email addresses you can communicate privately too. We recommend using your blog to drive email subscribers and then giving them first access to your latest content and new offers.

Guest blogging is a great way to build your profile and credibility.

However, eventually you'll want to build your own blogging audience.

Getting your first 1000 subscribers

Connecting with A-list and mid-tier bloggers is a skill that's integral to building your own blog. Jon Morrow from Boost Blog Traffic and Associate Editor of one of the web's biggest blogs, Copyblogger, is a brilliant example of what can be achieved when you know how the blogosphere works.

Unsurprisingly, the blogosphere mirrors real life in that it comes down to who you know as much as what you know.

Guest blogging increases your visibility

Through his video series, Jon Morrow shares his story of getting his first 1000 subscribers through guest blogging. Writing a guest post for a widely read blog puts you on the map, and on the radar of other key bloggers, giving you the credibility you need.

His guest blog posts drive traffic back to his blog via his author byline.

Whenever we were close to giving up, we'd have a 'hit' on our blog that generated unprecedented traffic, backlinks and shares. What was going on? What contributed to this? And how could we replicate it? It turns out that all the 'greatest hits' on our blog have followed a similar trajectory, and the writing itself plays only a small part.

How to write great headlines

David Ogilvy famously declared that, on average, eight out of ten people who are exposed to your content will read the headline, but only two of those will actually read the article.

Headline writing is paramount to the success of your content creation efforts. Why? Readers judge from your headline whether or not your content is worth clicking on. Think about your email inbox, your Twitter stream, your RSS blog feed, your Facebook or LinkedIn newsfeed, or even the first page of Google results. Your brain is constantly processing information, and judging it on the headlines alone. The best headlines are clicked; the rest is skipped over and lost.

Michael Hyatt, author of *Platform: Get Noticed in a Noisy World*, and Darren Rowse, founder of ProBlogger, both advise that you should spend as long on the headline as you do on the article itself. These two writers have monthly audiences numbering in the hundreds of thousands and millions, and they know how important headlines are to their success.

Brian Clark, founder of Copyblogger, has written one of the best free online resources on headlines, *Magnetic Headlines*. Jon Morrow wrote the other:

52 Headline Hacks. David Garfinkel has written the best book on headlines, *Advertising Headlines That Make You Rich*. A collection of the most effective headlines ever written, it suggests plenty of different ways to repurpose them for your own writing.

The best headlines work. When you next pass a newsstand take a look at the headlines on the covers of magazines. Review your blog feed and see what headlines jump out at you. The world's best writers know how to use headlines to capture readers' attention—that's why you'll see combinations of them everywhere.

Purists may criticise this technique for being unoriginal, but the best creative writers copy the best headlines. Some even say that's why they are called copywriters. Remember the words of Apple founder Steve Jobs: 'Good artists borrow, great artists steal.'

This is exactly what Adam did with a guest blog post for StartupSmart. He worked on 10 different blog titles, all from David Garfinkel's book, and after much deliberation chose 'Do you recognise these seven marketing sins?'

What's the best shortcut to learning effective headline copywriting? Head on over to your favourite blogs, go to the 'Most Popular Posts' and see how you can repurpose them for your own headlines.

For example, the most popular post on Michael Hyatt's blog is 'Advice to First Time Authors'. This can easily be repurposed to 'Advice to First Time Accountants', 'Advice to First Time Swimming Coaches' or 'Advice to First Time Marathoners'. Pretty easy to get into the habit, isn't it?

> ### Pro Tip: Comment on other people's blogs.
>
> This is the best way to pop up on other bloggers' radars, and a great way to be an active part of the broader blogging community.

The anatomy of a good blog post

Following are the main components of a good blog post:

- *Title/headline*. Your headline is where 80 per cent of people will stop. If it doesn't appeal to them and stand out in the flood of content in the reader's inbox, tweets or RSS feed, then your blog post will go unread. That's why it's so important to put a lot of thought into your headline.

- *A compelling opening sentence*. This needs to encapsulate what the article is about and draw people to read on.

- *Social media share buttons*. These are commonly found on all the best blogs. They enable readers to share the post with the click of a button, and also provide social proof that other people have found the article good enough to share with their networks.

- *Subheadings*. Your subheadings are important because most readers scan articles. Once people have decided to click through to your blog post, they should be able to pick up the gist of the article by scanning the subheadings. Make them compelling, so your reader will delve deeper into the content.

- *An image*. You know a picture is worth a thousand words. A picture also makes your article more interesting. It shows up in your RSS feed and on your blog home page. Ideally use an original photo that you've taken, or find one that you have permission to use and attribute it properly.

- *A call-to-action*. This is an element many marketers overlook. If you've done the hard work of writing a headline to attract your reader and you've delivered an interesting article that your reader has found useful, give them the chance to learn more if they are ready. Invite them to download your flagship content.

- *Your details*. As a content marketer, you need to make yourself and your business accessible so your readers can find out a bit more about you. You may prefer to keep your email private (to avoid spammers too), but your Twitter account or LinkedIn profile and your blog are perfectly fine to share and allow readers to reach you if they want. If you've impressed them with a thought-provoking article, you may well find yourself with new guest blogging offers, prospective clients and opportunities you never thought possible. Please ensure you link to your Google+ profile and have Google Authorship enabled so that your headshot will appear alongside your article in search results.

- *Comments*. Most bloggers have comments open on their blog. This allows readers to share their thoughts on the article. It also allows you to interact with your readers and extend the value of the post. You need not reply to everyone, but it's good to show your face.

It's good web etiquette to be visible and active in the comments section of your blog.

Download the Blog Post Planning Template from www.bluewiremedia
.com.au/blog-post-planning-template.

> ### Pro Tip: Set the house rules (or 'dinner party rules') for your blog comments.
>
> Let readers know that you value their input, but any malicious, defamatory, off-topic or spam-like comments will be deleted and the writer will be asked to leave.

A blog post shared with 47 000 CEOs

Toby is a regular reader of Verne Harnish's Weekly Insights email and religiously reads the books that Verne recommends. As Bluewire Media's CEO, Toby also has a keen interest in our team and 'hiring, retaining and working with A players', which was the topic of a book Verne was recommending. The book is *Topgrading* by Randy Street and Geoff Smart, and, as we do, we implemented what we could straight away and blogged about it.

As a courtesy and to show our appreciation, Toby emailed Verne to thank him for the book recommendation and point him to the blog post he'd written about 'How to create scorecards for Topgrading' (www.bluewiremedia. com.au/blog/2013/02/how-to-create-scorecards-for-topgrading).

We would do all of these things anyway, but it was also somewhat strategic in that we knew it was timely for Verne, since the authors were also the keynote speakers at an upcoming leadership summit. We never asked for anything, but we were over the moon when Verne featured Toby's blog post in his weekly email to over 47 000 CEOs and business owners.

Promotion

What was the missing ingredient that we hadn't worked out? We'll give you the short answer. *Promotion*.

The longer answer is that you need to keep promotion in mind in everything you do. From a magnetic headline that people will naturally want to tweet, to lively comments that prove your blog isn't a ghost town, to getting social media shares that spark an influx of traffic to your blog. It's all possible, and we didn't even need to change what we'd written.

We realised that it wasn't our blogging that was the problem. It was how we promoted our content once it was written. The problem was that as soon as we hit Publish, we thought our job was done. Not true. In fact, when we put in as much effort *after* we hit the Publish button as we did before, we had stellar results.

We like to write posts based on firsthand experience. Some of our more successful posts have been the Marketing Experiments series. It seemed to resonate because we were sharing the details of what we'd been experimenting with and revealing the results. We thought showing people 'behind the curtain' of our marketing efforts was more appealing than an article in which we'd preached at them.

How to promote your content

Once it's written and published, the promotion work begins, and the extra effort here means the difference between a 'hit' and a 'miss'. Unless you're an A-list blogger, it's up to you to get traction and keep the momentum going. Here's what we've found works well once you've published:

1 Email any friends or industry colleagues whose input you'd like in the comments. Chances are, they'll share it on their social networks too. With a few good comments under our belt, we'll email the blog post around our colleagues and invite them to share it with their networks (it's always up to them, of course!), and we'll include it in the weekly Bluewire News email.

2 If you mention anyone in the blog, it's polite to let them know via email or Twitter. If the article is good, you may get a few more tweets or social media shares; if you're lucky you may even attract a backlink.

3 Now your blog post is getting some attention and readers, you can start to promote it through your social media networks. Tweet it from your personal account and your company account. The same goes for Google+, Facebook, LinkedIn and Pinterest if you're on it. Submit your post to StumbleUpon and schedule a few tweets via Buffer to cater for followers in different time zones (folks on the other side of the world may be asleep, but you'd like them to see it). Maybe even try a few different 'tweet headlines' to see which version resonates best. You'll know from the number of retweets and favourites, and this can guide your headline writing in future.

> ## Pro Tip: Promote your post to new readers by adding it to LinkedIn Groups.
>
> These are groups of professionals with a mutual interest, like the 'Inbound Marketers' group Adam belongs to. As a member of these groups, you can start discussions by adding your content to the group conversation. As with IRL (in real life) it's rude just to show up, push your content on people and leave. Being an active member of the group and interacting in the comments can be very effective.

This step-by-step process is outlined in the Content Marketing Promotion Template, and it works just as well for blog posts as it does for premium content. Download the Content Marketing Promotion Template from www.bluewiremedia.com.au/content-marketing-promotion-template.

ProBlogger's Darren Rowse and his Digital Photography School blog

Some blog posts start off slowly and build momentum over time. For example, in the first year of his Digital Photography School blog, Darren Rowse wrote some articles that were 'slow burners'. They were useful articles but they didn't go viral. Over time, Darren gradually linked back to them from other articles, and hundreds of other websites linked to them over the years. The blog averaged only 150 views per day when it was first published in 2007, but has had more than 2.4 million views to date. Figure 9.1 shows this build-up in graph form.

Figure 9.1: Growing traffic for a 2007 post by Darren Rowse

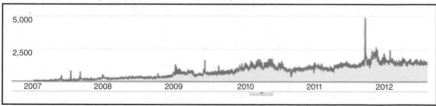

Darren comments, 'The other key lesson is that growing traffic to your blog is not always about trying to write shareable content that might go viral. This post is just a simple article that attempts to serve my readers. It wasn't written with growing traffic in mind—rather *it was written to serve my current readers*.' (www.problogger.net/archives/2013/10/10/5-first-year-posts-that-led-to-over-6-million-views)

Blogging is important in itself, but for business owners what is even more valuable is evolving this into content marketing. The key to graduating from blogger to fully fledged content marketer is having a system in place to grow leads and make sales.

Unfortunately selling still has negative connotations. If you prefer, look at it not as selling but as delivering even more value to people who want your help.

Are you a content marketer or a blogger?

What we've learned on our own web marketing journey is that there is a huge difference between simply blogging, where you are looking to grow a community of engaged readers, and content marketing, where you are actively looking to attract visitors and then convert them into leads and paying customers.

Blogging is a core activity in content marketing, but what we're talking about in this book is taking the steps needed to become content marketers—that is, adopting a defined process for attracting visitors, converting leads and closing sales. You can certainly be a blogger without being a content marketer. The vast majority of bloggers are hobbyists, but we need you to realise that the way to drive business results is to use your blog to attract leads and customers, not just readers.

Table 9.1 explores the main differences between content marketing and blogging.

Table 9.1: Key distinctions between blogging and content marketing

Bloggers...	Content marketers...
create and publish remarkable content that serves their audience.	also include calls-to-action at the end of their posts, inviting readers to take the next step and download a free resource via a purpose-built landing page. This allows content marketers to grow their email subscription list.
love comments and shares.	love conversions more. If a post goes viral that's brilliant, but it's even better if lots of those readers also convert into leads and, better yet, customers.
write purely for their audience.	also understand how Google works and how much new traffic it can send you. They write for their reader first, and for Google second. They perform keyword research to identify topics that have high search volume and low competition, and then they write content that satisfies this need.
like their content to spread.	strategically and proactively set about sharing their content by following a set process each time.

Summary

→ Blogging takes time, effort and a strategic approach, but the results can be huge if you stick with it.

→ Network with bloggers.

→ Write guest posts.

→ Killer headlines are crucial.

→ Promote your posts and syndicate them with other blogs to maximise your exposure.

→ Always include a call-to-action for your premium content to drive leads.

Tools and templates

Blog Post Planning Template
www.bluewiremedia.com.au/blog-post-planning-template

Content Marketing Promotion Template
www.bluewiremedia.com.au/content-marketing-promotion-template

WordPress powers over 20 per cent of the world's websites, so you can't go wrong getting a Wordpress.org blog setup and paying to have it hosted on your domain.

Gravity Forms and add-ons 6 (from $39)
www.gravityforms.com/add-ons/

Buffer
www.bufferapp.com

Stumble Upon
www.stumbleupon.com

WordPress plug-ins (free):

Jetpack for social shares
WordPress SEO All in One plugin by Yoast

Disqus plug-in for blog comments

Dashboard Commander

Magnetic Headlines
www.copyblogger.com/magnetic-headlines

52 Headline Hacks
www.boostblogtraffic.com/headlinehacks

Advertising Headlines That Make You Rich by David Garfinkel

Chapter 10

Video, audio and image publishing: YouTube, webinars, infographics and podcasts

A picture is worth a thousand words.

Proverb

As soon as our mentor Mike showed us the Flip Cam, we knew we had to get one. By hitting one big red button, you could shoot high-definition video and upload it straight onto YouTube by flipping out the USB connector. Too easy. No more excuses.

We bought our Flip Cam and started filming short videos of ourselves explaining how we could help, and interviewing people we met. Mike helped get the ball rolling by giving us one of our first expert interviews, and we continued to record interviews with business and marketing experts, racking up more than 60. We took our Flip Cam everywhere we went, in search of great interviews. Of course, these days you can record HD quality on a smartphone.

YouTube—a no-brainer

When you think about the fact that most people would rather watch videos than read, and that YouTube is the second largest search engine in the world, it was a no-brainer for us. And the web was full of stories of Gary

Vaynerchuk's rise to fame with his daily wine videos for Wine Library TV and Tom Dickson's Will It Blend YouTube series.

Learn from our blunder: Adam & Toby's 'suggestive' YouTube video

If you've ever had to watch a video of yourself you will know that it's excruciating! If forced to endure such agony, as we were, you are unlikely to make it to the end of the recording because you get so self-conscious. We've filmed quite a few videos for our website, and the main one has always been on our home page. We titled it 'Adam & Toby—Welcome to Bluewire Media'.

Twelve months later we were having an initial consultation with a prospective client. After a fairly successful first meeting, the company's marketing manager said he didn't approve of our home page welcome video, and if we didn't change it he wouldn't be able to engage Bluewire. We were shocked! We asked why and were told they were a family-friendly business, and we should watch the video to the end.

Needless to say, we raced out of the meeting to rewatch our video. At the end, YouTube had provided its list of 'suggested videos' based on our description. Within seconds we discovered that 'Adam & Toby' is also a series of erotic videos. Once our video was over, our home page suddenly became a quasi-porn website—which certainly wasn't the look we were going for. We changed the settings to disable the suggested video feature and that company went on to become one of our best clients.

Video content is so easy to produce

Smartphones have quality inbuilt video cameras, and if you want to go even more pro you can buy a Handycam and a tripod for under $500. Of course you can spend more money, but really the idea is to get started on filming and uploading your videos. Blaming a lack of resources for specialised equipment is honestly just a stalling tactic.

Overcome the fear of publishing your content and get it out there!

Pro Tip: Consider using an autocue program.

If you are prone to forgetting your words or you want to make a more professional impression, use the free EasyPrompter tool (www .easyprompter.com) or buy the Teleprompt+ for iPad app for $15.99. Adam's preference for talking-head videos is to use an autocue because it allows you to focus on *how* you deliver the content rather than remembering your lines. Yes, you are an expert and you know your stuff thoroughly, so you may feel you don't need one, but your videos will be a lot sharper if you're focused on your presentation and looking at the camera.

What software do you need?

Software-wise all you need is Screenflow, iMovie or Windows Media Player to edit your videos, and these programs will automatically upload them to YouTube for you. If learning the iMovie basics is too daunting, never fear. Post a job on freelancing websites like oDesk or Elance and outsource it to a video professional to take care of it for you.

Tips for producing great interviews

Here are some tips to set you on your way to delivering great interviews:

- *Use Skype to conduct remote interviews with experts.* With free Skype and the $29.95 Skype Call Recorder, you have the technology to interview anyone who agrees to your request. Distance and time zones are no longer barriers to filming an interview, and since guests can do interviews from the convenience of their own home or office, we've found a very high strike rate. Skype Call Recorder lets you split the screen to show you and your guest next to each other on the recording. The sides of the images are cropped, so take care to sit in the middle of your screen.

- *Audio is most important, so invest in a microphone.* The Blue Yeti, the podcaster's mic of choice, will set you back about $150. Not only does it improve the sound quality, but you'll look and feel like a radio DJ.

Bad audio ruins a video, whereas bad camera work or poor lighting is just an inconvenience.

- *Seize opportunities to interview interesting people in person.* Attending a local event or a conference is a great opportunity to connect with speakers or fellow attendees and bag a five- to 10-minute video interview. It's as easy as finding a quiet corner with adequate light and recruiting someone to hold your smartphone and hit record.

- *Have your videos transcribed.* Using SpeechPad, which costs as little as $1.00 per minute of audio, you can achieve near-perfect transcripts of your videos. This is ideal for blog posts or web pages because you give people the option to watch or read the content. Reading is generally much faster than watching and readers can go at their own pace, scan or re-read bits, and skip ahead. An added benefit is that it provides more relevant content for Google to index, and you have the option of repurposing videos, especially interviews, into e-books.

- *Make sure your music is royalty-free.* If you're using music, you'll need to source royalty-free tunes to avoid any copyright issues. Unfortunately you can't just run your favourite track from iTunes in the background. The sites we use for royalty-free music are Looperman.com and MusicLoops.com.

Table 10.1 sets out some practical dos and don'ts for the interviews themselves.

Table 10.1: dos and don'ts of video interviews

Do...	Don't...
face natural light where possible	use fluorescent lights—they make everything flicker
prop your laptop or webcam so it's at least head high	look down into the camera—it's unflattering and viewers will be looking up your nose!
nod and smile	make polite noises while your guest is speaking. In face-to-face conversations you give verbal cues to show you are interested and paying attention, but on video a background stream of 'hmm, u-huh, yeah' is distracting.
allow pauses to let your guest finish their story	talk over your guest
check out how you look before you start. You need good light and should be dressed appropriately.	wear stripes—they go blurry on screen
perform a test run with a colleague to check internet, camera, mic, audio and Skype Call Recorder	waste your guest's time
provide a good introduction and opportunity for the guest to say how viewers can get in touch or follow them	forget to turn off your phone and your Skype notification sounds. Let the interviewee know you are completely focused on them!

Should you reveal what questions you are going to ask?

We prefer not to reveal our questions beforehand because we find the interview flows a lot more naturally that way. Some guests prefer to know them in advance as a condition of interview. We always mention what topic we'd like to cover but ask the questions for the first time during the interview so the answers are more spontaneous. That said, Adam does prepare his questions in advance, though he keeps the agenda open so he and the guest can go off on a tangent if the opportunity presents itself.

> ## Pro Tip: Shine the light on others.
>
> Use your videos, podcasts and webinars as a way to give exposure to other people in your industry. Be generous, and amazing things will happen. Eventually you'll find that reciprocal opportunities will open up for you.

Screencasts

Using Screenflow for Mac or Camtasia for PC, you can easily record how-to videos and share your screen with the viewer. This is particularly useful if you are either shy or want to get really detailed.

Mr Likeable

Adam knew of Dave Kerpen as the chairman of Likeable Media, CEO of Likeable Local, best-selling author and the most trafficked LinkedIn influencer in the world, with more than 2.4 million views. He received Dave's company's Likeable newsletter offering his new book as a free download on Kindle for a few days only, and asking for readers to share it with their friends. Adam got it, enjoyed it, reviewed it and, as requested, shared it with our 8600 subscribers. He dropped Dave a note to pass on that he'd shared the book, and was chuffed when he actually wrote back:

> Wow, thank you so much, Adam! I so greatly appreciate it! Let me know what I can do for you please. You rule! —Dave

This led to a recorded Skype interview a few weeks later, and a connection with one of our aspirational contacts. It was totally unexpected and not what Adam was setting out to do, but generosity has a way of being reciprocated.

Webinars

A webinar is like a seminar but is super convenient for speaker and guests alike since it's all done via the web rather than in person. Conducted from your desktop or laptop, it's a cheap alternative to an in-person event. Plus you can communicate your message with people all over the world. Adam's first webinar was with the American Marketing Association, and he used exactly the same slides as he would in an in-person presentation.

Audience members can ask questions by 'putting up their hand' electronically, whereupon the moderator can switch their mic on.

The only disconcerting thing with webinars is that you can't see the audience's reactions, so it's hard to gauge whether you are pitching it at a level that is too advanced or too basic, or even whether they are enjoying it! Aside from that it is a very effective communication medium. And because everyone is at their computers, if you finish your presentation with a call-to-action, it's very easy for the viewer to follow through by subscribing, downloading resources, connecting with you or buying a product. Use paid tools like GoToWebinar or free tools like Google Hangout On Air.

> ### Pro Tip: Address audience members by name.
>
> As the host of a webinar you can see all the attendees' names on your dashboard. It's easy to make attendees feel the love by reading out their names. It makes everyone feel special!

Infographics

We posted our first infographic about a LinkedIn 5 Minute Daily Marketing Plan, and after modest promotion it had over a thousand views within a week. We followed the process in our Content Marketing Promotion Template and soon our infographic was published on Hubspot's popular blog as well as dozens of others. This generated thousands of views and shares, plenty of backlinks and hundreds of new leads, really highlighting how popular this visual type of content is. It was a successful first experiment and led to a series of 5 Minute Marketing Plan infographics.

The rise of Pinterest and Instagram has seen a huge increase in the amount of web content that is image-based. If a picture is worth a thousand words, an infographic is worth 5000. Try taking a short blog post or list and getting it designed into an infographic. We were surprised by how much information you can actually fit on an infographic, and how incredibly popular they are. People love to retweet them, pin them on Pinterest and embed them in their own blogs (and you earn a backlink).

View the LinkedIn 5 Minute Marketing Plan infographic at www .bluewiremedia.com.au/blog/2013/11/linkedin-marketing-strategy -infographic.

Podcasting is here!

Podcasts that you host on your website, on iTunes or on SoundCloud are easy to record. A mic and a recording program such as Garage Band (for Mac) or Audacity (for PC), and you're away.

A podcaster who has burst into prominence is John Lee Dumas, who hosts the daily podcast Entrepreneur On Fire. That's right—every day. John interviews a mix of big names and under-the-radar guests. Adam had the pleasure of being guest number 92 on his show and has followed him ever since.

Getting started

John Lee Dumas's Kindle book *Podcast Launch* provides full instructions on how to get started and how to get podcasts onto iTunes, but the real challenge isn't technology, it's overcoming self-doubt. When Adam interviewed John for our blog, he explained that 'imposter syndrome' was the biggest challenge he faced when starting out in podcasting, but he overcame it by thinking of himself as simply the conduit for the guests' ideas.

If you're not a writer

John was a very enthusiastic communicator but preferred to talk rather than to write. Podcasting appealed to him because he saw the blogging world as a marketplace that was crowded with people who were already well established. The podcasting world, though, was much less crowded, with plenty of 'blue ocean' opportunities—especially with the iTunes marketplace accessible to everyone with a smartphone or internet connection. No one was doing a daily podcast for entrepreneurs, so after his aha! moment John decided to seize the opportunity.

After that he set out to secure his first handful of guests, and he did this by attending the BlogWorld conference in 2012. He networked with some high-profile bloggers and asked them if they were willing to come on his show as his first guests.

Getting traction

John's success can be attributed to the colossal effort required to prepare and release one podcast per day, and to his diverse range of guests. He has selected a format that works for him—a set series of questions that he asks all guests. He's got a tight schedule and keeps a few weeks ahead of real time. He also encourages listeners to leave five-star reviews and dedicates a section of his show to cheer on those who do. The number of five-star reviews is used by iTunes to determine which podcasts earn a place in its 'What's Hot' section.

In the first eight weeks of a podcast, John recommends making the most of being in the 'New and Noteworthy' section. The more five-star reviews you can muster, the more chance you have of graduating into the 'What's Hot' section after the eight weeks are up.

Profitable business on its own

The day Adam interviewed John he had just published his revenue and profit figures for the previous month—a staggering $88 978.08 in profits after just 14 months of podcasting. His month's download figures had grown to 450 000, so he had built a very decent-sized audience.

Let's take a look at where this money came from. Remember, these figures were for *one month*.

> Sponsorship of the show: $39 345
> Mentoring: $6000
> 'Mastermind' membership website: $13 500
> 'Podcasters Paradise' membership website: $35 787
> Affiliates: $5075
> After expenses: $88 978.08 profit

Aside from monetising the podcast itself, marketers and business owners position themselves as trusted advisers, experts in their field, retaining existing clients and at the same time growing their audience and increasing the likelihood of attracting new clients.

Summary

→ Video is now very easy to produce. You can do in-person or Skype interviews, film yourself on a smartphone or Handycam, or record screen-share videos.

→ These can be hosted for free on YouTube.

→ Get your videos transcribed with SpeechPad so you've got a written version of the content too.

➔ Webinars are very effective because people can watch them from their computer.

➔ Infographics can bring high visibility to your content, especially since they are so popular on Pinterest.

➔ Podcasting has really taken off, but it is still not as crowded as blogs. If you prefer speaking to writing, start a podcast.

Tools and templates

Content Marketing Promotion Template
www.bluewiremedia.com.au/content-marketing-promotion-template

Skype Interview Template
www.bluewiremedia.com.au/skype-interview-template

Instagram 5 Min Marketing Plan
www.bluewiremedia.com.au/instagram-daily-marketing-plan

Pinterest 5 Min Marketing Plan
www.bluewiremedia.com.au/pinterest-daily-marketing-plan

Skype (free)
www.skype.com/

Skype Call Recorder ($29.95)
www.ecamm.com/callrecorder/

Screenflow for Mac ($99)
Camtasia for PC ($99)

SpeechPad (from $1 per minute of audio or video)
www.speechpad.com

Entrepreneur on Fire
www.entrepreneuronfire.com/

Pat Flynn's Smart Passive Income YouTube channel (watch his eight-part free podcasting tutorials)
www.youtube.com/user/SmartPassiveIncome

Cliff Ravenscraft Podcast Answerman YouTube channel
www.youtube.com/user/cliffeotc

GoToWebinar
www.gotowebinar.com

Google Hangouts On Air
www.google.com/+/learnmore/hangouts/onair.html

Podcast Launch by John Lee Dumas

Chapter 11

Publishing content and finding your editorial rhythm

On the web, you are what you publish.

David Meerman Scott

When we started email marketing in 2006 it was all we did, but we did it consistently every month. Then in 2008 we started blogging, and we stuck at that. We're actually quite grateful that all the social media networks hadn't exploded onto the scene in our early years because it would have been easy to have spread ourselves too thin and lose focus.

As YouTube, Facebook, Twitter, LinkedIn, Instagram, Pinterest, Vine and even SnapChat burst into our lives, we had the luxury of learning each of them as they came of age. You don't have that luxury any more, though, and many of our clients have felt overwhelmed, not knowing where to start.

This is totally understandable. There's only so much time in each day, and business owners have plenty of responsibilities other than those around creating content. How do we know where to focus our attention to get results and not waste our time and money? We get the problem.

We also appreciate that *knowing* what to do is much easier than actually *doing* it. We all know we *should* exercise and eat well, but that knowledge doesn't make it any easier to get up and go training or avoid that tasty but unhealthy dish. It's no different when it comes to content creation—it's very easy to do nothing.

If you've read this far, you know the importance of content and you're driven to take action, so let's take a look at where and how to get started.

Build around your flagship content

Take your flagship content and build your editorial calendar around it. Ideally everything you do in your blogging, guest blogging and social media helps build trust and guides people towards your flagship content. Remember, it should be placed on a landing page where visitors register their name and email address. This helps you build your opt-in email subscriber list, and lead-nurturing takes off from there.

For example, a direct approach is to tweet about a blog article, which someone will hopefully click on and read. If you've provided a good article with a call-to-action at the end of it, a number of those readers will take you up on the offer to download your flagship content in exchange for their email address.

A less direct approach is to share other people's valuable content on social networks and deliver value to your followers. When you do this you'll build trust and the number of your followers will increase. Then the next time you share your own blog posts more of your followers may click through, read the post and convert on the flagship content page.

Picture your buyer personas

First things first. When you sit down to draft a tweet, post a Facebook update, write a blog post, film a video or record a podcast, it's always handy to picture your buyer personas (see chapter 2). Picture them as you create the content and deliver it, as if they were the only people receiving your advice.

When Adam writes he often imagines our buyer persona Nicola; he thinks of the challenges she faces and how Bluewire Media can address them. He writes, or speaks, as if he is speaking directly to her, and his goal is to be as useful to her as possible. Unless he is sharing firsthand experiences, he will write in the second person, which means using the words *you* and *your* a lot. That way his readers feel like he is writing directly to them, which he is.

Writing and creating content

There's no real secret to this. It takes practice but we're all capable of creating remarkable content. Everyone has an individual style and personality, and since there is only one you, the best advice is to be yourself and speak naturally. Write a blog post and send it off to your email subscribers to see what sort of response you get. When your work resonates and you get good feedback, continue to refine it; when things fall flat or you get no traction, see how you can improve — or try something else.

These three tools are especially useful for blog writers:

- Evernote is great for taking notes on the go and then revisiting them when you're back at your computer ready to create.

- Feedly is a blog reader that makes it easy to follow all of your favourite bloggers without having to visit them one by one.

- WordPress is the most popular blogging platform. We find it easiest writing straight into WordPress.

Getting into the habit

The people who get the best results from social media plan out what they'll be publishing and how frequently, and then have a system for holding themselves accountable for producing and sharing their content. What makes it into your calendar is real and gets done. A well-planned schedule comes to life when you save time for it each day.

The secret to success is simply practice, persistence, some discipline and a little bit of luck.

Keep creating content and the quality will improve over time, and be disciplined about publishing it regularly and promoting it. Most people give up way too soon.

Once you have your strategy and your flagship content worked out, here is a rough guide to implementing it. The aim is to be consistent in the way you approach your editorial calendar. Of course there will be times when you do more or do less, but creating these habits will help keep you on track.

Finding your content rhythm

Here is a useful guide to get you started, but you'll soon discover your own rhythm.

Daily

- Scan your favourite blogs for inspiration and to get your imagination going. We use Feedly so all the blog feeds are in one place. It's convenient to set this up on your smartphone, so you can also read them when you're on the run.

- Share via social media two or three useful articles that your followers may find interesting. Be sure to mention the author of the content, because it's good manners and so they know you're sharing it. You can use Buffer to pre-schedule these updates on Twitter, LinkedIn, Facebook and Google+.

- Check your LinkedIn messages. Adam started checking these messages daily after he missed out on a social media speaking engagement because he was too slow. Learn from his mistake!

- Jot down any ideas for blogs, videos or premium content in Evernote.

Weekly

- Publish a blog post once a week. To make it easier, refer back to the ideas you've jotted down in Evernote during the week and then flesh out your article in the time you've set aside to write it.

- Whenever you publish a blog post, remember to save an hour or so to promote it online. Follow the 20 steps in the Content Marketing Promotion Template, and share it with your network via email and social media.

- Write an email newsletter that keeps your community up to date with your latest news, useful articles and any other valuable content you can share with them. The golden rule is always to deliver lots of value.

- Leave a thoughtful comment on one or two of your favourite blogs. Get into the habit of doing this, because it's a great way to connect with people and build relationships, and it shows you're contributing and getting involved.

- Connect with five people you know on LinkedIn using LinkedIn's 'people you may know' feature. You can now also save information such as how you met and important dates.

Fortnightly

- Write a guest blog post. Find fellow bloggers or websites whose audience may be interested in what you can contribute. They get fresh and valuable content for their readers and you get in front of a new group of people, and gain a backlink. Always be respectful, educate them and put a call-to-action at the end so interested readers can find out even more by heading over to your website.

Monthly

- Upload a Facebook photo album from an event you've been to or from a company get-together. These photos personalise your business so potential clients and staff can get a feel for what you're like.

- Write a LinkedIn recommendation for someone and also request a recommendation from a client you've worked for. A LinkedIn profile with genuine endorsements is a lot more powerful than testimonials published on your website, which cynical people are reluctant to believe.

Quarterly

- Send a sales email. Invite your readers to purchase a product or service from you. It could be an event, an hour's consultation, or a digital or physical product. It's important to encourage people to buy your products and to overcome any potential fear of selling online.

- Film a YouTube video. It could be an industry update or a how-to video. If you're a bit shy, you could always interview an expert or get a video testimonial from a customer. Record it on your phone or laptop camera and edit it in iMovie or Windows Movie Maker, and you're away.

- Run a webinar. Your community of subscribers and followers will be eager to draw on your expertise, and a webinar is an easy way to teach them new things from the convenience of your computer.

Annually

- Write an e-book. Aim to write at least one new e-book every year. Not only will this improve your writing, but it will help you clarify your thinking and condense it into a more concise form. There are few better ways to demonstrate your expertise and earn the trust of your potential customers.

- Conduct a customer satisfaction survey using a Google Form or Survey Monkey.

- Ask what your audience would like from you. This can guide the content you deliver and the products and services you create.

- Release premium content, such as IP you use internally, a market report, interviews with thought leaders, metrics reports or survey data. Add these to your library of premium content that we recommend you include on landing pages!

The Editorial Calendar Template and Social Media Planning Template are frameworks that will help keep your content publishing efforts on track. Download them from www.bluewiremedia.com.au/editorial-calendar-template and www.bluewiremedia.com.au/social-media-planning-template.

Congratulations. You have just become a publishing house. Recall the words of David Meerman Scott: 'On the web, you are what you publish.'

You are very nearly there. All you need to do now is remember to follow the 20 steps in the Content Marketing Promotion Template. When you publish a blog post, video or other premium content, take about half an hour to promote the content through your social networks, especially LinkedIn Groups, and via email. Reach out to people you've mentioned in the content or who have helped inspire it. Otherwise it's a waste of your effort to create quality content.

How to generate content

To help keep it exciting and to avoid the overwhelm of a 'blank canvas', it's useful to make a note of all the various content ideas that you and your team have. Store them all in a collaborative space like a Google Doc or Basecamp project to make it much easier when it comes time to create content.

Here's a great activity for your team: using sticky notepads everyone writes down content ideas for each of your buyer personas. Everyone can write or paste their suggestions up on a whiteboard or wall. Then you can record all these ideas in the Editorial Calendar Template, and even let certain people allocate ideas to themselves. Whenever you come to write, pick a topic from the list and away you go!

Getting started on creating *new* content

Here are three suggestions for getting started on creating new content:

1 *Answer every question.* Draw up a list of every question any customer has ever asked you about your product or service. Answer them all as blog posts (or you can use video responses and have them transcribed with Speechpad.com). Often you'll find a number of themes emerging from the questions and answers. Group them together either as a whole or as separately themed e-books. The side benefit of this is that you will be solving your customers' problems using their language, and you will compile a powerful collection of content and keywords for the search engines too.

2 *Do you have any research or product reports?* If you generate research as a part of your business, use it and share it. Compile it into a form that is useful for your buyer personas.

3 *Interview experts.* The beauty of expert interviews is that you will eventually be 'guilty by association'. Many an interviewer has achieved the same high visibility and status as her guests merely through association with so many experts. There will be no shortage of people to interview, and you can do it in person or via Skype. The transcripts make great content for your blog as well as e-books. Remember to keep the interviewees in the loop if you decide to publish the interview on your blog or as an e-book. It's good manners, but also a good excuse to share the love and strengthen your relationships. You'll also benefit from the kudos of having been the interviewer—you'll be seen as the curator of great information—and the growing trust of your audience.

For more ideas on what to create, download the Content Ideas Generation Template from www.bluewiremedia.com.au/content-ideas-generation-template.

> ## Pro Tip: Give people what they want.
>
> Through our marketing experiments we have found our content, in order of popularity, is (1) templates and tools, (2) e-books, (3) feature blog posts, (4) expert interviews, (5) photos.

A word of encouragement (or warning, if you want quick results)

> Ask your physician how to feel good, and he'll look you in the eye and say, 'Eat right and exercise.' Yet for every dollar spent on fitness, Americans spend nineteen dollars on cocaine. The reason? Two seconds after you snort cocaine you feel like Superman. Two weeks of diet and exercise just makes you feel sore. — Roy H. Williams, *The Wizard of Ads*

Likewise, marketers get hooked on paid advertising because, as soon as you spend money, you see your ads everywhere and feel like Superman. Two weeks of content creation leaves you exhausted. Paid advertising is like a drug: it's expensive, addictive and leaves you chasing the next high until the money dries up. However if you're prepared to do the work, and stick around for long-term results, the approach in this book will catapult you past your competitors.

There are good habits to get into and techniques for amplifying your efforts. Let's just get started, take baby steps and build momentum from there. You really are building a marketing asset one brick at a time. Just pick a place to start, and start.

It is relatively simple to become a great content marketer, but it takes time and persistence. The reason most people don't get there is that doing nothing is easier. Chasing shortcuts or instant results is more appealing.

Creating content can be great fun, especially once you've found the platform that suits you best.

> ## Pro Tip: March to the beat of your own drum.
>
> As you build momentum, and discover the joys of creating content, you will most likely diverge from the 'rules of thumb' we've outlined and blaze your own trail. The most successful people online prove there is no set rulebook, and in fact the more you push to the edges the more success you are likely to find. It's really up to you. The only things that matter are that your audience finds your content valuable and that they trust you!

Different strokes

Timothy Ferriss blogs roughly once a week and delivers epic, multi-thousand-word posts that really dive deep into practical how-to. Tim is very active in his comments and also interacts with his community on Twitter. By contrast, Seth Godin blogs every single day without fail. His posts are often very short and pithy, but he doesn't have comments on his blog, nor does he interact with people on Twitter. These two approaches are at opposite ends of the spectrum yet both are fantastically successful.

Similarly, Chris Brogan authors nearly all the posts on his blog, whereas Brian Clark and Darren Rowse open up their blogs for guests to share their insights. All three are among the web's most trafficked and high-profile bloggers, but they take different approaches.

Something else you will notice when you study people who do web marketing that works is that many will opt out of certain platforms entirely so they can focus their efforts on the handful that are most enjoyable and effective for them.

Summary

→ Build your editorial calendar around your flagship content.

→ Write content for your buyer personas.

→ Find your daily, weekly, fortnightly, monthly, quarterly and annual content publishing rhythm.

→ Use the Editorial Calendar Template to keep your publishing on track.

→ Generate a list of content ideas to overcome the 'blank canvas' overwhelm.

→ Settle on the style, frequency and platforms that work best for you — and march to the beat of your own drum.

Tools and templates

Social Media Planning Template
www.bluewiremedia.com.au/social-media-planning-template

Content Marketing Promotion Template
www.bluewiremedia.com.au/content-marketing-promotion-template

Content Ideas Generation Template
www.bluewiremedia.com.au/content-ideas-generation-template

Content Publishing Rhythm Template
www.bluewiremedia.com.au/content-publishing-rhythm-template

Editorial Calendar Template
www.bluewiremedia.com.au/editorial-calendar-template

Evernote
www.evernote.com

Feedly
www.feedly.com

WordPress
www.wordpress.org

Buffer
www.bufferapp.com

SpeechPad
www.speechpad.com

Part V

Getting found

Chapter 12

Search and keywords:
search engine optimisation

Don't build links. Build relationships.

Rand Fishkin

In 2008 we were unfindable on Google. We told ourselves it didn't matter because word-of-mouth referrals were the best way to attract more customers. We told ourselves that our strong email list was better. It wasn't growing quickly, but it was about 2000 people.

To be honest, we just didn't understand how Google worked. So we focused on other things that we knew better. That all changed when we Googled 'web design Brisbane' and couldn't find Bluewire Media in the results. Not just on page 1, or page 2. We clicked through the first 10 pages, and saw nothing but tumbleweeds ... and competitors.

If, as the saying goes, 'You are what Google says you are', we were nothing. We were embarrassed. Embarrassed that we couldn't be found, and that we didn't know what to do about it.

So we decided to turn it around.

Adam is the kind of marketer who loves a scoreboard with which to measure his work. Email open rates, new subscribers and web traffic are all numbers he follows like a hawk. Now that our ranking, or lack thereof, for 'web design Brisbane' was on the scoreboard, he applied a laser-like focus.

First he needed to learn how search engine optimisation (SEO) worked. Naturally he turned to Google, and he started learning. The resource that kept jumping out at him was an e-book called *SEO Secrets* by a fellow Australian, Glenn Murray. According to the blurb and reviews, it offered 200 pages of no-fluff, actionable SEO steps that even non-techies could follow. Glenn's endorsements were top notch, so Adam dived right in.

He didn't regret it. In fact, he loved it. Of all that he'd seen and read, it gave him the best appreciation of how Google worked.

How Google works (for a non-techie marketer)

Adam learned that Google is always looking to deliver the best results to the searcher.

A simple rule of thumb is that if you 'write great stuff' Google will reward you with high rankings and visitors.

This truly is valid advice and has served us well ever since.

Of course there's more to it than that, and a slightly more detailed explanation is needed to understand how the Google juggernaut works.

What Google wants

While little is known about the specifics of the Google algorithm, we do know Google is specifically looking for two things:

1 **Content that matches what the searcher is looking for.** Your website must be relevant to the search word or phrase. Obviously, if someone is searching for 'financial advice', then your website will need to include those two words. Otherwise Google won't know what your website is about. Of course there are hundreds of thousands of other finance websites out there too. To outrank them, your site needs more than just the search term 'financial advice'. It has to have 'authority'.

2 **Evidence of how much authority you have.** The most authoritative and relevant web page in any given field ranks first on Google. The next most authoritative and relevant ranks second—and so on

down the list. The most important factor contributing to Google's assessment of your authority is the quality of the links pointing to your website. These are called backlinks. In Google's eyes, every backlink is a vote of confidence, an indication that your website is credible and useful. Links are the currency of the web, but did you notice we said 'quality' rather than quantity?

A backlink from a very important site is worth more than hundreds from low-quality sites.

Google also picks up on other cues, such as your social media influence and the popularity of your content on social networks. Your backlinks typically reflect your relationships—but more on this shortly.

But SEO is still the Wild West

The SEO industry is notoriously full of cowboys. It doesn't help that our inboxes are spammed with offers from SEO companies promising to propel us to #1 ranking for any given search term. In our experience, many of these companies cannot themselves be found on Google, other than appearances on 'RipOff Report'!

But despite the huge number of sharks, it is pretty easy to separate the wheat from the chaff—by doing a simple Google search on them. You'll find that reputable SEO companies can definitely help make your website 'visible' to search engines. They can make sure it's technically up to scratch, that your content is written so that Google can 'read' and 'understand' it. They can help you decide what searches you want to rank for (and thus which 'keyword phrases' are best to write content around). They can even help you get backlinks.

However, you know your industry best and are the expert on your subject. Plus you know the people in your industry, so the advice we give marketers and business owners is to create your own content and build your own online networks, rather than outsource these.

What reputable SEO companies won't do is make promises about how long it will take, be secretive about their methods or tell you they know how the Google algorithm works. If you hear any of that, run!

Determining what people are searching for

The first step with SEO is to decide what words or phrases your buyers are searching for in Google. The simplest but often most overlooked way is to ask customers what they typed into Google to find you. This will help you to see things from your buyers' perspective.

Google Instant

Another super easy way to see what people are searching for is to start typing a phrase into Google. You'll notice that as soon as you start to type, Google will suggest four or five different searches you might like to try based on the letters you've entered.

For example, when we were researching the name for our 'editorial calendar', we started typing it into Google, and the Editorial Calendar Template came up as the first suggestion (see figure 12.1).

Figure 12.1: Google Instant and the 'editorial calendar' search phrase

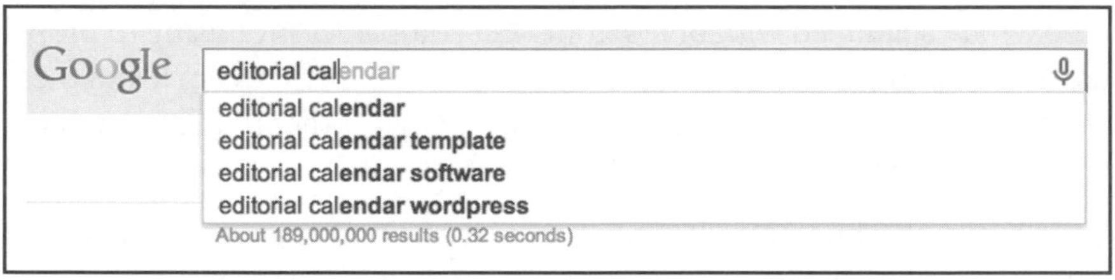

Google and the Google logo are registered trademarks of Google Inc., used with permission.

Similarly, when we typed in 'content calendar', the first suggested phrase was 'content calendar template' (see figure 12.2).

Figure 12.2: Google Instant and the 'content calendar' search phrase

Google and the Google logo are registered trademarks of Google Inc., used with permission.

What is this telling us? What's happening is Google is making suggestions based on what has been a popular search phrase with other people. If you use these words to inform your title, you know that it is a search phrase that people are interested in. This is a very easy way to research keywords and proof that you are optimising for a phrase that's popular.

In the example of our editorial calendar, we decided to name the page Editorial Calendar Template (Content Calendar). This way it is very clear what the tool is, and it incorporates both the keyword phrases that Google indicated were popular. In Australia, this tool ranks on the first page of Google and has been our third-best performing landing page, generating more than 100 new leads every month. If we hadn't taken the time to name the tool appropriately, we would have missed this opportunity.

Übersuggest

Übersuggest is an awesome free tool that makes the task even easier. It pulls in data from Google Instant. For example, when we were working out the copy for the Editorial Calendar Template page, we used Übersuggest and it gave us the following suggestions:

- editorial calendar template excel
- editorial calendar template free
- editorial calendar template download
- editorial calendar template for social media
- editorial calendar template for google docs
- editorial calendar template
- editorial calendar template 2012

We then knew we should add the words *excel*, *free*, *download*, *google docs*, and *2012* (except we made it *2014*). Figure 12.3 (overleaf) shows how we've incorporated all those keywords into the web page.

Figure 12.3: incorporate keywords into your web page

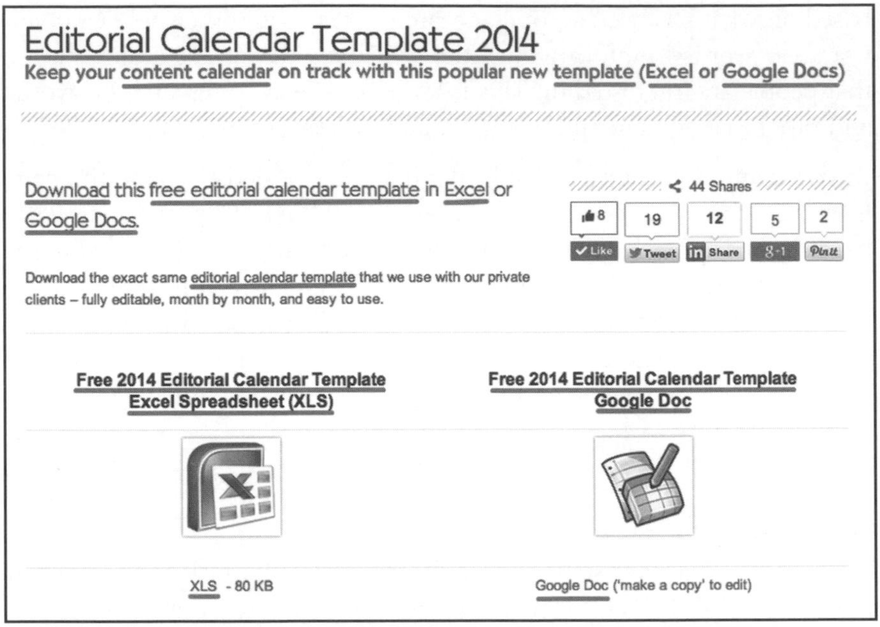

Pro Tip: Optimise your landing pages.

It's common practice to consider SEO when you write a blog post, but in our experience the best conversions take place when people in search of a template click directly on one of our landing pages.

Incorporating keyword phrases

In the good old days (late 2013), Google actually provided very useful data with its Keyword Tool, but unfortunately for SEOs it's now decided to encrypt much of this information in its renamed Keyword Planner.

Back when we had this data at our fingertips, we learned that the best keyword phrases for converting visitors into subscribers nearly always contained the word 'template'. It made sense. You could imagine that someone looking for a template would probably be in a proactive mindset, intent on taking action, so they were more likely to download something given the option.

It may not make sense for you to create a template (although we advise you to think hard before dismissing the possibility), but the point is you should be trying to create tools that people will be able to use, tools they're desperate for. Then optimise your landing pages accordingly.

Optimising your site: basic on-page SEO

Now you know what you want to rank for, you need to make sure your website is cleanly coded so Google can access it properly. This is known as on-page SEO. Each page is labelled appropriately so Google knows what it's about. It can get a little technical, so if you find yourself out of your depth this is where an SEO professional can add the most value.

The basic components of a web page

URL: the actual address of the page (usually www.something). When choosing your URL, try to include descriptive keywords, preferably words your customers are searching for. This tells visitors and Google what the page is about. For example, www.bowesfitness.com/free-half-full-marathon-training-programs/ is way more effective than www.bowesfitness.com/page-10.

Page title: the name of the page that appears on the browser tab, as well as in the title in Google search results. Definitely include keywords here.

Page description: the snippet that shows up in the Google search results

Main heading: (tagged as <h1> in the code) specifies for Google what the page is about. Ideally your keyword phrase is contained in the title.

Subheaders: (tagged as <h2>) help Google evaluate what the page is about. The subheaders decrease in priority after <h2>; it's a good idea to ensure they are consistent at each level.

Body copy: the main text of the article itself that the visitor is here to read. Don't stress about optimising these words because you'll have included the keywords and phrases in the title and headers. If you're obsessed with getting keywords into your writing, the copy will become 'keyword stuffed' and less engaging to read. Always write your content with human readers in mind.

(continued)

The basic components of a web page (cont'd)

Alt text: (alternative text) identifies your images. For example, 'image. jpg' is an unhelpful description for an image, whereas 'Sean-Bowes-Marathon.jpg' conveys useful information to Google. (Vision-impaired people also rely on alt text to discover what an image is. They use a screen reader to read out the alt text, so you want it to be useful.)

Anchor text: the visible, clickable text in the link itself. ('Sean's marathon program' is better than 'click here to visit the page'.)

Internal linking: the practice of linking to other pages within your website, which also helps Google understand what your website is about.

Download the SEO Planning Template from www.bluewiremedia.com.au/ seo-planning-template. If you go it alone, a word of warning: a little bit of knowledge can be dangerous. It's easy to get caught up in anchor text, meta tags, alt tags or whatever the latest SEO technique is. Our advice is, don't. It's a deep vortex that compels you to fiddle around incessantly and unnecessarily. Instead ...

Focus on creating killer content and on strengthening your relationships within your industry.

Getting good backlinks: basic off-page SEO

Off-page SEO is everything relating to your site that happens off site; mainly it comes down to backlinks. As we suggested earlier, think of this as relationship building rather than link building. Talk to suppliers about linking to you, and talk to industry bodies about links. Do the groundwork to build up a solid base. Start doing a few guest blog posts. Short of publishing content so amazing that top bloggers or journalists choose to link to it, guest blogging is the best way to earn high-authority backlinks.

The best but also the most challenging way to get backlinks is to publish truly remarkable content that people choose to link to without your needing to ask.

A great blog post can attract a multitude of links within days of being published.

This takes effort, skill, promotion and a dose of luck, but it is the best way to increase your authority.

Another off-page consideration is the number of social media shares you get on your website, such as when someone tweets your page. Google will certainly see that as an indication of your website's authority.

> ### Pro Tip: Don't go chasing the Google algorithm.
>
> Google's top-secret algorithm is under lock and key, like the Coke recipe, but it doesn't matter. Google is smarter than any one of us, and to attempt to game its rules is madness. Because of Google's secrecy, some SEO professionals will create a lot of fuss every time the company releases another algorithm update (such as Panda, Penguin or Hummingbird). They will claim there are new opportunities or new things to fix. Our experience, however, has been that every time a new algorithm update is released our ranking improves, or at the very least it stays the same. Google rewards great quality content, so if you simply stay focused on that goal, Google will catch up and rank you accordingly. The only people who get worried about or punished by algorithm updates are people who have acted unscrupulously. If your ranking has suffered a sudden drop, it's worth getting a reputable SEO to help.

How to gauge domain authority

A lot has been said about specific websites' authority but how do you actually assess this? The best free tool to use is called the Moz Toolbar. You can add it as a web browser extension, and the free version will reveal the following information:

- *Website data: domain authority (DA).* ___/100, based on ___ inbound links from ___ (number of) domains

- *Web page data: page authority (PA).* ___/100 (indicates the authority of a specific web page, as opposed to the website overall)

- *MozRank:* ___/10 (an exponential rank that indicates the relative strength of the page, so a MozRank of 8 is 10 times better than a MozRank of 7).

Just Google 'Moz Toolbar' + your preferred web browser, such as Chrome, Safari or IE).

Open Site Explorer (another Moz product) will also list your backlinks and calculate the domain authority of each. The free version will give you the total number of links and specify the first five linking domains. To extract all the information you need a paid Moz account, which costs $99 per month. If you're serious about SEO, this is a wise investment.

Provide tools that people can use, and optimise them accordingly!

Link building is really relationship building

It's somewhat crude and misleading to refer to the practice of attracting inbound links as 'link building'. The phrase itself has negative connotations—think link farms, dodgy SEOs and other all-round 'black hat' behaviour. Think of it instead as relationship building. People who know, like and trust you are more likely to link to you, and are more likely to let you write a guest blog post for them.

When 37signals blogged about wanting customer testimonials, we jumped at the chance. Why? Aside from the fact that we loved them, the main reason was because their website has so much authority that a backlink to our website would pass on a massive amount of trust. In SEO jargon, it had heaps of Google juice or link love! In fact, the 37signals website has a domain authority of 70 and remains one of our most important backlinks.

Pro Tip: Ask for testimonials.

Work through your list of suppliers (especially software suppliers) and approach each to ask if you can write them a testimonial. Most will then include a backlink to your website.

'Web design Brisbane' vs 'social media speaker': optimising for customers (vs traffic)

The ego-nourishing high of our top ranking for 'web design Brisbane' gradually faded as we found that none of these leads converted to customers, let alone best customers. In fact, this keyword phrase attracted tyre kickers who were mainly price shopping, and never bought from us. We soon learned this from our analytics, and also from asking our clients.

On the flip side, we discovered that our best clients were finding us via the key term 'social media speaker'. Our clients, we realised, looked to work with thought leaders and experts, and searched accordingly. Typically after engaging us for a paid speaking engagement, they'd discover that we also offered web strategy and web marketing services. This was a major revelation, and we focused our optimisation efforts accordingly.

The lazy marketer's guide to SEO

Unless you've been slapped by a Google algorithm update, there's no real need to get caught up in all the Google updates and what SEO professionals are banging on about. As a time-poor marketer, you would be better served by focusing on looking after your buyers with remarkable content.

Certainly get the basics in place so Google indexes your website properly, and understand how it all works, but after that, relax. If you're an ethical and effective content marketer, take solace in the knowledge that you will continue to be rewarded for your good work, no matter what updates Google introduces.

Summary

→ Search engine optimisation is all about telling Google what your website is about.

→ Google ranks you according to your content and authority.

→ The first step is to decide what your buyers are searching for, by doing some research.

→ Make sure your website is coded correctly so Google can read and understand your content.

→ Then focus on good-quality backlinks and relationships to improve your authority.

→ You are better off focusing on creating great content for your buyers than worrying about the latest Google algorithm updates.

Tools and templates

SEO Planning Template
www.bluewiremedia.com.au/seo-planning-template

Google+ 5 Min Marketing Plan
www.bluewiremedia.com.au/google-plus-marketing-plan

Google Instant
www.google.com/instant

Google Keyword Planner
https://adwords.google.com/ko/KeywordPlanner/Home

Moz Toolbar
moz.com/tools/seo-toolbar

Open Site Explorer
www.opensiteexplorer.org/

SEO Secrets by Glenn Murray
http://bluewi.re/SEO-Secrets-e-book

Übersuggest
www.ubersuggest.com

Chapter 13

PR on the web: influencer outreach

No one ever succeeds without the help of others.

Jay Abraham

Getting that mention in a major publication or from an A-list blogger can really boost your credibility and give you a burst of top-quality traffic. It can provide the visibility and influx of readers to launch you to the next level. Most of all, it's great validation of your content.

Unfortunately it is very hard to arrange at short notice. An entire industry, public relations, has been built around helping businesses get this type of coverage. Historically, PR agents cultivated the crucial relationships and harvested their little black book of contacts. It was their job to lobby and pitch to journalists, reporters and bloggers on your behalf. The power lay in the strength of the relationships they had built up, and of course they would charge you handsomely for the privilege.

The good news for web marketers today is that we can now forge these relationships ourselves. Thanks to Twitter, email subscription and LinkedIn, we can now build up our own little black book of contacts and, more importantly, nurture these relationships. We simply need to invest the time and take a strategic approach.

About PR

Securing attention when *you* want it is fraught with hazards, especially if you haven't first built up years of credit. Crafting press releases, and conceiving 'angles' for stories, involves a set of skills that PR professionals acquire over time. If this approach works for you, please keep doing it. Sometimes you'll have a great story but lack the right relationships or contacts to get it out there, so a PR agent can be of huge value to you.

But there is a different, more cost-effective approach that circumvents these gatekeepers. This approach is better suited to today's business owners and marketing managers. By investing your time rather than your money you can open as many doors as you are brave enough to knock on!

Getting PR in the social pages

At Bluewire we've written only four press releases, and each resulted in top-quality publicity. We were highly targeted and had done our research. We held Bluewire birthday parties and invited a handful of media contacts to attend. We had our heart set on getting featured in the social pages in the *Sunday Mail*, Queensland's weekend paper.

We followed traditional PR techniques, sending an email (with no attachments!) to the appropriate person at the newspaper, explaining the party we were going to throw. Fortunately, the combination of guests, time of year and venue piqued their interest enough for them to send along a 'shooter' to get some photos.

Aside from those four press releases, every single one of our other fifty-plus press mentions has resulted from 'inbound PR'—journalists, producers, authors and bloggers approaching us. Some were more luck than strategy, others the opposite. We did a few things that we highly recommend.

Getting lucky

We've been fortunate enough to be referred by friends and found on Google. Everyone has their share of luck—some good, some bad. Our good luck included being referred by a friend for an interview in the *Sydney Morning Herald*. The reporter was a freelance writer called Ali Cain who we'd got to know by keeping in touch and inviting her along to our events. We had surfing in common and became friends.

Before long this relationship led to a speaking engagement on a marketing panel at the National Small Business Summit, which was exciting because we were the curtain-raiser for the next speaker, none other than the current Prime Minister, Tony Abbott. These things tend to snowball, and one of the other panellists was Valerie Khoo, author of *Power Stories*, who became a valued adviser and friend. We took her 'How to Write a Business Book' course at the Australian Writers' Centre, which led to the book you are now holding.

Everything is connected and the more you get involved, the more serendipitous things happen and the more generosity you encounter. For example, Ali became a full-time writer at Fairfax, and this led to Adam's first published newspaper article.

One of the things we have discovered is that relationships have a funny way of paying you back.

A reporter with whom we did a phone interview in the early days became another ally, at the same time proving the power of Twitter. Journalist Alex Tilbury and Adam spoke about social media in an article for *The Courier Mail*. Adam was singing the praises of Twitter to a newbie, so Alex agreed to give it a go. She signed up and they followed each other. A few months later Adam was running his first marathon on the Gold Coast along with 5500 other runners, and at the 7 km mark just south of Broadbeach he heard, 'Hey, I know you! From Twitter. You're Adam, aren't you!' Bloody hell. On his left, there was Alex herself, who was running her first marathon too.

They'd never met and knew each other's face only from Twitter. What a great way to meet! With 35 km left to run, they had plenty of time to bond. They actually ran most of the race together, until Adam's competitive blood started pumping and he tried to break away with 7 km to go. He was too cheeky and overconfident, and maybe Alex was understating her training, but despite Adam's mini-breakaway Alex soon caught him up and tapped him on the shoulder as she overtook him with 500 metres to go. Serves him right, huh!

Their legs slowly recovered, and Alex and Adam became fast friends. Not long after, Alex was promoted to Chief of Staff at *The Courier Mail* and was kind enough to speak at our Web Strategy Summit. The world is a small place and it's amazing how things pan out.

People end up in all sorts of interesting places

One Bluewire News subscriber worked at a marketing firm in Brisbane, and we got to know each other via the newsletter. A few years later she moved to Sydney and became a sponsorship manager at McDonald's. With her new marketing budget, she engaged our firm to work on a very exciting project.

Be generous and kind to everyone in your community. Be grateful that people want to learn from you and have put their hand up to be associated with you. Knowing you've helped someone is a great feeling, and that alone is enough to keep us jumping out of bed each day to do the things we love. Anyone can become a fan of your work and a referrer, and you never know who is going to be the next decision maker at a company you'd love to work with.

Marketing is a long-term game built on long-term relationships. So we've learned not to be concerned with chasing down Oprah, CNN or *Forbes*. Get to know the people in your network, serve them well and don't expect anything in return. Then wait to see what twists of fate help you on your journey.

Reaching out

Reaching out to leading bloggers can be daunting, especially when you consider how big their audiences are and how often they get approached by would-be guest bloggers. But we have found that they are actually very approachable — provided you're sincere. Aside from being social creatures, most bloggers are interested in getting to know their readers, increasing their readership and gaining new customers. In our experience they have also been happy to support people in their tribe.

These are the 10 steps to take before you ask to increase your chances of success:

1   Identify the influencers in your market.

2   List them in a spreadsheet.

3   Follow them on Twitter.

4   Read their blogs.

5   Comment on their blogs.

6   Tweet and share the posts you like.

7   Subscribe to their email newsletters.

8   Reply to their email newsletters with generosity and sincere praise.

9 Buy their books, read them, review them and blog about them.

10 Remember: lead with generosity and form a relationship before you ask for anything but it works even better if you don't explicitly ask.

> ## Pro Tip: Don't ask for anything.
>
> Influencers know you'd love a retweet or backlink or endorsement. If it's good enough, they'll do it without your having to ask.

When it's time, download the Blogger Outreach Email Template, at www. bluewiremedia.com.au/blogger-outreach-email-template, available at the end of the chapter and as a guide on how to proceed. If you don't get a reply, don't hassle them, and don't give up either! Go back to the 10-step process, and try again later. Keep being generous and helpful, and you'll get there eventually.

Hat tip to Rand Fishkin and Timothy Ferriss for paving the way here!

So rather than be like most other people and go around hassling bloggers when we want something, we spend months, often years, following their work and getting to know them.

Aspirational contacts

For us, part of this process was compiling an Aspirational Contacts list, an idea inspired by relationship and networking expert Keith Ferrazzi in his book *Never Eat Alone*. Every time we heard or read about someone interesting in the marketing or business arena, we'd enter them into our Google spreadsheet and add in more information. We'd follow their blog via Feedly and subscribe to their emails. We'd really immerse ourselves in their work, digest it and get very familiar with it. This strategic approach can take years, which is why it works so well. Anyone looking for quick hits usually takes the lazy scatter-gun approach, which gets you nowhere.

So we'd follow them on Twitter, subscribe to their emails and read their books. We'd absorb as much about them as we could, and our first interaction would always be one of gratitude.

The idea is to be purposeful and strategic in how you approach it, and to lead with generosity.

If you are manipulative, insincere or acting only out of self-interest, it won't work for you. If, however, you identify people whose work you admire, and with whom you genuinely want to form a long-term relationship, the strategy works well.

Our goal has been eventually to invite aspirational contacts to be interviewed for our blog and YouTube channel. The reason this has worked successfully so far is that we are offering to spread their message to a new audience, namely our 9000 email subscribers. It takes only 10 to 15 minutes out of their day, and can be done from the comfort of their home or office via Skype.

For us, it's really exciting and fun because we get to chat with them, to learn from them and to share their messages with our audience. It makes for great content, so we repurpose the YouTube video by embedding it into a blog post with the transcript. Or we'll take a series of videos and transcripts and turn four or five interviews into e-books.

The bonus is the perceived credibility of interviewing these influential people. And, though we never ask for it, there's also the occasional backlink, tweet or blog mention once the content goes live, which connects us to their audience too.

Download the Aspirational Contacts Template we use from www.bluewiremedia.com.au/aspirational-contacts-template.

Wait, you stalk them?

You could suggest that jokingly (or to cast scorn on our approach), but it doesn't really do it justice. Building relationships takes years, and sincerity and appreciation are not qualities that can be faked for that long.

The web allows us to connect and form meaningful relationships with people virtually anywhere. Twenty years ago you met people because you had mutual friends or you shared the same geography. Now you can connect with people who have the same interest as you regardless of where they live in the world. Never before has this been possible.

Ice-cream with Chris Brogan

We're now in a hire car on our way to meet Chris Brogan, one of our favourite bloggers and an aspirational contact. Sure, it took years and flying halfway around the world to make it happen, but it was totally worth it.

Like web marketers and bloggers the world over, we were well aware of Chris Brogan's work and his stature in the blogosphere. When we knew we would be heading to the US to attend and speak at a few conferences, we made a special effort to get to Massachusetts, where, according to Twitter, Chris lived.

The big names in blogging have readers all over the globe and probably get hit up all the time. Nevertheless, in true Timothy Ferriss, comfort-challenging style, Adam decided we should try to meet the man. He wouldn't have attempted this if he hadn't been part of what Chris calls his 'Monchu', his tribe. He read his weekly newsletters, followed the blog and had exchanged a few emails and tweets. Hardly close mates, but he took inspiration from Chris's book *Trust Agents*, in which Chris said it was always nice to encourage up-and-coming bloggers or, as Adam says, people further down the food chain—and we were certainly that.

So after Chris's open invitation arrived while we were in Boston, we hired a car and drove several hours to share ice-cream with him!

Don't (necessarily) take no for an answer

Sometimes persistence pays. We'd tried a similar approach to meet with Brian Solis in Silicon Valley, California. The email came back: 'No, out of town. Sorry.' We weren't deterred. In our travels in California we noticed a meet-up hosted by the Altimeter Group, and it seemed like a good idea to turn up and mingle with our fellow web folk. To our surprise, there was Brian Solis, so Adam went on over to say hello.

He didn't ask for anything, and didn't bail him up for long, but he had initiated contact, and they had connected over a shared love of the Bondi Icebergs, based right near our home in Australia. Another win!

Grow with your media contacts

The best way to approach media relationships is to keep in mind the old adage: *Lead with generosity*. If you're brand-new and looking to get your business on the map with some publicity, don't spend your time trying to get chummy with the editor of *Forbes* or that producer from CNN, and don't go knocking on Oprah's door. Instead, get to know the up-and-comers who cover your industry. Track them down on Twitter, follow them, tweet their material and leave thoughtful comments on their articles.

One of the best things about Twitter is it's a means to connect directly with the journalists who write about your industry. We keep a Twitter list of journalists who cover social media, marketing and web-related businesses, so we get real-time tweets from these people and can keep a finger on the pulse of what they are writing about.

One morning Adam saw a call-out from a reporter who was looking for a comment from email marketers. He tweeted back and was sent a couple of questions to comment on. He quickly sent back a short email reply, and it ended up being used in *Business Review Weekly* and syndicated in the *Financial Review*, two of Australia's leading business publications. No PR agency, no press release—just the real-time tool Twitter to stay connected with the influencers in our industry. Opportunities like this abound if you are open to them. As David Meerman Scott says, 'Social media are the tools, real-time is the mindset'!

Owning the ink

In a short interview with *BRW* magazine, Toby stated that one of his goals was to write a marketing book. It has been a goal of ours ever since Verne Harnish advocated that you need to 'own the ink' in your industry.

When we were researching how to write a book, we went straight to the blog of one of our favourite marketing authors, Seth Godin, to see what he had to say about it. Number two on his list of advice to authors is to start marketing the book three years before it comes out. So we did.

We grew our blog, we guest-blogged and we grew our subscriber list. We also started forming relationships with bloggers in our industry, and learning from them all. Part of getting on their radar was buying their books, reviewing them, implementing what we'd learned and dropping them an email to thank them. We followed the process with our aspirational contact spreadsheet, and continually added more names to it.

Getting this book deal

When we came across books we really loved, we'd buy copies for our clients and subscribers. We've bought hundreds of our favourite books, written by our aspirational contacts, through various publishers. One benefit of this is that it marks us out on the author's radar because we ask them for signatures. Most authors happily oblige with a book signing if you are buying their book in decent quantities. We'd learn that authors are always keen to promote their books, so once we'd initiated contact we'd ask to film a Skype interview for our blog and Bluewire News. Most would agree, and we'd promote them to our subscribers.

Since we'd also been interviewing several Wiley authors and promoting their books on Bluewire News, our contact at Wiley, who we bought our books through actually emailed us to ask if we'd considered writing a book ourselves. Wow, what timing!

We'd been planning to write a book, and were building towards doing it and *bam*, there was an email from a publisher we'd secretly dreamed of working with. We were soon introduced to the commissioning editor and given the opportunity to submit a book proposal.

We'd be dumb to discount the element of luck here; nevertheless it came after three years of growing our blog, readership and contacts, as Seth had advised, and being generous with our promotion of other authors in our niche. Of course, buying hundreds of books from Wiley over the years would've definitely worked in our favour.

Sending handwritten cards and thank-you cards

Part of Verne Harnish's 'Rockefeller Habits' checklist is sending one thank-you card per week. Dave Kerpen, *New York Times* bestselling author and chairman of Likeable, also recommends sending thank-you notes on a regular basis. And sales coach Jack Daly sings the same song. For many years we've both carried around a 'card and note pack' with us.

We also try to keep track of the birthdays of aspirational contacts, friends, clients and colleagues, and at our weekly meeting we'll see whose birthday is coming up and send off a card. Additionally, whenever we've met someone interesting, or been helped by someone, we express our gratitude by sending off a thank-you note or card.

In a web-enabled world, the power of a handwritten, snail mail–delivered card is huge. Add it to your arsenal.

Pro Tip: Create your own cards.

We used to have our cards customised via SendOutCards and push out 'picture cards' with photos we had taken. The only problem was we couldn't actually handwrite in them. You typed in what you wanted to say and it was printed up for you and sent directly to the recipient. We preferred to write notes in our own hand. One day Angela in our office baked a batch of cupcakes and decorated them with Bluewire-coloured icing. She took a photo of the stunning result, and that picture now adorns the front of our original card.

We keep Bluewire Media branding to a minimum; in fact, aside from the colours in the photo, it's non-existent. There's just a company sticker on the envelope. It takes a bit more effort to make these cards, but feedback proves it to be well worth it.

Blogger Outreach Email Template

> ## Pro Tip: Let the blogger know
>
> This works best when you've established a relationship and if you don't explicitly ask for anything. They know you'd love a re-tweet, backlink or endorsement. Your job is to bring it to their attention and if it's good enough, they'll do it without you having to ask.

Blogger Outreach Email Template

Part	Example	Why it works
[Greeting]	Hi Toby,	It's personal and friendly
[Personal introduction and sincere praise]	I've been a fan of your blog since I was referred to it by a friend in 2012. -----or----- Your recent write-up in the _____ publication caught my attention, and it prompted me to reach out to you.	It shows you know, like and trust them.
[Lead with generosity]	Your blog post about _____ resonated with me so much that I emailed it to our 9,217 subscribers and tweeted it to my followers. -----or----- I love your new book. I bought a copy and left this 5 star review on Amazon.	It shows you have already been generous to them. The law of reciprocity.
[Tell them]	I've just written this blog post sharing 10 things that I learnt from you. http://bit.ly/10things	It is short and simple.
[Ask] (this part is optional)	If you felt it was worthy, I'd love a retweet, (but of course I understand if you don't.)	It's direct but gives them an out too.
[Close]	Anyway, I really just wanted to say thanks. I also see you'll be speaking in Australia soon. If you get time for a surf when you're in Sydney, try to make it to Bondi — it's a great beach!	It shows you are helpful, attentive and thoughtful.
[Your details]	All the best, Adam **Adam Franklin** @Franklin_Adam Marketing Manager, Bluewire Media www.BluewireMedia.com.au	It allows them to do their research on you or jog their memory as to who you are. It lets them see if you are legit!

Pro Tip: Don't give up

If you don't get a reply, don't hassle them, and don't give up either! Go back to the 10-step process, and try again later. Keep being generous and helpful, and you'll get there eventually.

Hat tip to **Rand Fishkin** and **Timothy Ferriss** for paving the way here!

Summary

→ Getting mentioned by influencers is a long-term game.

→ Business owners and marketing managers can build direct relationships with journalists, thought leaders and bloggers with time and a genuine approach.

→ Growing and nurturing your network is crucial to creating PR opportunities on the web.

→ You never know where someone will end up, so be generous and genuine with everyone.

→ Take the time to get to know your aspirational contacts. Get involved in their communities and build a relationship — long before you might need it.

→ You can't fake sincerity and appreciation, so don't try.

→ If you can't get in touch through one medium, try another. Offline is often the least crowded.

→ Grow with your media contacts.

→ Send handwritten thank-you cards.

Tools and templates

Aspirational Contacts Template
www.bluewiremedia.com.au/aspirational-contacts-template

Blogger Outreach Email Template
www.bluewiremedia.com.au/blogger-outreach-email-template

Chapter 14

The secret to online is offline: events and speaking

You can use tradeshows to network with people who would otherwise never return your email or phone call.

Timothy Ferriss, on his *The 4-Hour Workweek* book launch

At the Social Media Down Under conference in Sydney in 2013 we invited 13 speakers to share their stories. No one likes a hard sell at a conference, so we focused on delivering value, and guest speakers did the same. At the end of the day we handed out feedback forms to see how we might improve future conferences. One attendee wrote, 'We'd love to work with Bluewire on our social media'. The next morning they had a proposal in their inbox, and they signed off within two hours. That was a five-figure piece of work, straight off the back of a live event, with no selling.

All the strategies laid out in the previous chapter can be maximised by meeting people in the flesh. Rather than badger them for meetings, which can be a lot of effort, especially if the groundwork of generosity hasn't been done, a great approach is to go to conferences to meet speakers and fellow delegates.

There are plenty of conferences around Australia and overseas. Our rule of thumb is if there are two or three aspirational contacts on the speaking card, then the event will be worth attending. When we found as many as 10 aspirational contacts on the program for Inbound12 in Boston, we packed our bags. The flights cost six times the conference ticket price, but it was worth it.

Inbound12: making the most of the opportunity

Hubspot's annual conference for inbound marketers was the first fully fledged US-style conference we'd attended. A conference is considered a big hit in Oz if you get 600 people in a room. Try more than 3000 people, and in only its fourth year!

Faced with this large number of inbound marketers, we had our work cut out tracking down the people we wanted to meet. We also looked forward to making new friends along the way.

The main thing that differentiated us was the fact that we'd flown halfway round the world to be in Boston, and we were two of only three Aussies at the event. We'd loaded a backpack and maxed out our legal quota of Australia's finest Bundaberg Rum—in 200 mL bottles. We filled the remaining bag space with packets of chocolate TimTam biscuits. With this bait, we were fairly sure we'd cater to most people's vices.

One of the drawcards of the conference for us was the calibre of speakers and delegates, especially those 10 aspirational contacts—people whose blogs and books we'd read, and who we'd long hoped to meet in person. We often give out marketing books to our Bluewire News readers, clients and event attendees, so we thought it would be cool to get some signed books to bring home.

Given the luggage allocations, logistically this wasn't going to work too well. Then we realised we could take stickers to be signed then add them to the books when we returned. At the conference we enjoyed chatting with these authors for a few minutes as they signed the stickers.

If we were really lucky, and it felt appropriate, we'd ask if we could also do a quick two- to three-minute Flip Cam interview. (Now you'd just use an iPhone).

Attend events to meet people

Aside from meeting aspirational contacts, attending events is incredibly valuable because of the other attendees you meet. The speakers' content will mostly be available for free on YouTube. Speakers like Seth Godin, Gary Vaynerchuk and Jim Collins charge multiple tens of thousands of dollars for a keynote, but most of their talks are available for free on YouTube.

Which means that the real value of a conference lies in the people you meet and catch up with. If your sole purpose for attending an event is to hear the speakers, you should probably stay at home and watch them on YouTube. If you want to see an ROI for your financial outlay, talk to people. Don't flick your business card around the room to as many people as you can, but rather focus on having a few meaningful chats with people you'd like to follow up with.

Research who will be attending by looking at the event hashtag or, if it is public, the Eventbrite attendee list. Find out what you can on LinkedIn and Twitter about which people sound interesting to you, and reach out to them in advance. Introduce yourself, and suggest catching up for a coffee during registration or morning tea.

> ## Pro Tip: Organise your own 'tweet-ups'.
>
> At events with a tech-savvy audience, Twitter regulars will often congregate at the breaks for designated tweet-ups. You can easily organise one of these, but be very specific on where and when you'll meet and how people can identify you! Adam has been to an awkward tweet-up where he didn't know who had turned up for it and who just happened to be standing around.

Organise post-conference drinks at a nearby bar. Don't tread on the event organisers' toes, but if there's no official after-conference function, tell a few of the people who you're already connected with, and set a time and venue. Then spread the word to those who are interested. Aside from being a fun way to end the day, you get to know people that bit better, and since you organised it you get the kudos as host.

Organising live events

MarketingProfs' and the Content Marketing Institute's 2013 annual report cites live events as being the most effective content marketing tactic. We agree. The web and social media allow you to connect with people the world over, but getting people together in the flesh by hosting a presentation, workshop or a simple meet-up will help strengthen those relationships and build your authority.

However, there is a huge element of risk in organising your own event. There is a fear of embarrassment. What if you lose money? What if no one shows up? What if speakers let you down? What if you go to all this effort and it proves a waste of time? It's always nerve-racking waiting for ticket sales to come in and then waiting to pass the break-even point, but this inherent risk means there is less competition. If you can get people along to an event that's well organised and fun and also delivers useful content, you deserve to reap the rewards.

Events aren't for the faint-hearted, since they are so daunting. What follows are tips from our experiences hosting free parties, basic meet-ups, full-day conferences and $1000-per-person workshops.

How to run your own event

From a logistical point of view, Eventbrite and PayPal will be the tools you need to set up event pages and take care of ticket sales. Attendees can register and pay via their credit card and get an instant receipt, and the money goes straight into your PayPal account. If you decide to offer refundable tickets (which we do), it's really easy to issue refunds. You'll also be able to share the event via social networks and set up an event page on Facebook.

Choose a venue that can take care of all the catering, room setup and AV, because you'll want to maximise the time you have to press the flesh with your attendees. You'll have enough to worry about without dealing with caterers and technological issues. We usually recommend going for the premium food-and-drinks package as it makes a great impression and you can factor it into the ticket price.

Different types of live events

Live events take several different forms.

Before- or after-work seminar or meet-up

These may go for one to two hours and involve a presentation and an element of networking. If facilitated properly, the networking component should be at least as valuable as the presentation. Our favourites are marketing meet-ups—drinks and canapés while guests mingle with their marketing peers, putting faces to Twitter handles. We've chosen to price these events at between $30 and $80, and aim to attract 50 to 70 guests. Aside from being fun events, these meet-ups provide an easy first step for people to get to know you in person.

Full-day workshop

Some workshops are best held in a hands-on environment where everyone has their own computer and internet connection. Sometimes, if the workshop is more about strategy, it can be more rewarding to disconnect from the web and work through the day in small groups.

We price these events at between $800 and $1000, and prefer to cap attendance at 15 to 20. By limiting numbers, we can address the group's most pressing issues in more detail.

Should you organise a half-day workshop? If you can host the event at your premises then it's worth considering, but in our experience you're up for pretty much the same cost if you hire a venue for half or a full day. It's much harder for the venue manager to rent out a room for half a day after you've left, and if attendees need to request time off work, it's often as easy for them to get an entire day as a half day.

Full-day conference

Full-day conferences are fun because you get to invite an array of different speakers to share their stories. Hand-pick people you know or whose work you are familiar with so you can craft a really good program. A couple of lousy presentations can really suck the life out of your event.

Many speakers will relish the opportunity to speak in front of a new audience, and some higher profile speakers may charge a fee. If you use seasoned speakers, your audience is more likely to enjoy the day and you reduce the risk of putting them to sleep.

It is always good etiquette to thank your speakers appropriately.

Pro Tip: MC your own event.

As the event organiser you are the connection between the audience and the speakers, and stepping into the MC role cements this relationship on the day. Aside from hosting the day, there is credibility in speaking alongside your guests. If this totally freaks you out, engage an experienced MC but still remain visible, perhaps handing over the thank-you gifts.

Connecting people

In our web-connected world, the exciting part of live events is the energy of having everyone in the same room.

In fact, one of our best experiences has been to host an event where those people have known each other online for as long as five or six years but are meeting face-to-face for the very first time. It's common to hear, 'Hey, I've followed you on Twitter for years. How are you?' They know each other's kids' names, their hobbies and passions—all through social media. It's something like a school reunion, but they're meeting in real life for the first time.

> **Pro Tip: Invite media contacts and bloggers as VIPs.**
>
> It's an easy way to lead with generosity and show up on their radar. Don't make it awkward by asking the journalist to write about you, but if they do, be sure to express your gratitude. Of course, they may write about another speaker and not even mention you at all, but that's fine. In that case, you've connected two people and they've both benefited. That is good karma.

Should you run free events?

The argument for running events for free is to attract more people and hope that they become customers. However, the perceived value of these events is often low. At free events we've attended, there have usually been lots of no-shows, evidenced by the number of name badges left unclaimed on the registration table. People who haven't paid to attend are more likely to drop out. Also, free events often end in an uncomfortable sales pitch. It's awkward when they apply the hard sell, and this has never been the vibe we've aimed for.

Ironically I've found the less you 'sell', the more sales you make. Brian Clark of Copyblogger has always drilled into us that 'teaching sells', and that has been our approach.

The only free events we've run have been our annual Bluewire birthday parties. In putting on these celebrations, we've raised thousands of dollars for charity and garnered some good publicity, but above all we've been able to say thanks to the people in our community.

Public speaking

Ever since Grade 7, we've both enjoyed public speaking. That's not to say it didn't terrify us at times, but it has also been a big thrill. Jerry Seinfeld famously said most people would rather be in the coffin than giving the eulogy, but being on stage is the place you want to be at a conference. You may earn a speaking fee, but most importantly you will be seen as the thought leader and build trust with the audience. People are much more likely to buy from people they've seen and perhaps spoken with.

Prepare — then practise, practise, practise

To prepare a one-hour keynote, speaking professional and TED talker Nancy Duarte recommends spending 30 hours on planning the talk, 30 hours on creating the slides and 30 hours practising. This is a lot, but it's important if you want to get your speaking to a level where you get paid to do it.

If it's your first presentation, the golden rule is to practise, practise, practise. Practise out loud to yourself, then do it in front of a mirror, in front of family or friends, in front of your colleagues and then in front of a small business group. If you can, video yourself and play it back. This is one of the fastest ways to improve. Then do it for real.

Decide on the type of speaker you want to be known as — make it quite specific. It's also worth deciding on a phrase that the people hiring you will use. We created the speakers page on our website and optimised it for 'social media speaker'. The best way to do this is to ask event organisers to link to this page from your speaker bio section on their website. Our top ranking on Google has helped attract more than 100 speaking engagements around Australia and internationally.

It has become a source of revenue, earning us as much as $12 000 for speaking engagements.

Our best clients have seen us speak before hiring Bluewire Media.

This has become one of the best ways to attract leads and grow our community.

Speaking tips from 100 presentations

Here are our best tips gleaned from our speaking experience.

Beginners: be prepared

- Craft a presentation on a topic you are passionate and knowledgeable about. Weave together four or five stories you know well, such as case studies, firsthand experiences and funny anecdotes.

- Use slides with pictures, images or screenshots, and one or two words max. (Never have a slide full only of bullet points!)

- Print out your slides as 9 × 9 thumbnails, and jot down the stories you are going to tell at each point. These notes make it easy to refresh your memory when you get nervous beforehand, and make it easy to remember your content as you go. (Never write out and read your presentation word for word.)

- Know your first 60 seconds and last 60 seconds by heart. Everything in between will be fine because you know the stories and you'll relax into telling them.

- Carry a large (at least 16-point) printout of your introduction for the MC in case they forget theirs.

- Carry a USB with a copy of your presentation, and keep a copy on Dropbox or your email, just in case!

- Arrive early so you can test that everything works.

- Practise to ensure you finish on time.

- Take seven deep, slow breaths before you go on stage. Walk up. Pause. Look at four friendly faces in the audience. Away you go!

Intermediate: move around

- Get your own Logitech pointer with built-in timer that vibrates at 10 and two minutes to go.

- Move away from the lectern to stand directly in front of the audience.

- Walk among the audience occasionally.

- Include time for Q&A, and have a question up your sleeve in case no one puts up their hand. When faced with a deafening silence from an audience, start with 'A question I am often asked is ...' Then answer your own question to get the ball rolling.

- Never finish with 'Okay, no more questions? Thanks'.

- After the Q&A, deliver your prepared 60-second closing statement.

Advanced: introducing humour

Comedians tell us the easiest way to be funny is to tell stories you already know are funny. You'll have a handful of stories that you tell regularly to make your friends laugh. Some of these will be business-related stories, so find a way to weave them into your presentation.

For example, the story of Adam sending his 'Dear Adam' email to all 700 subscribers always gets a laugh, because the audience can relate to Adam's embarrassment.

Aside from real stories, our speaking coach taught us that humour is usually derived from the unexpected. If you present information in a pattern, break that pattern with the unexpected. For example, 'Who uses social media? Who's had some success with social media? Who's had social media go so wrong they've had to move to another country?' This one always breaks the ice.

Overcoming imposter syndrome

Every speaker has encountered this feeling. The internal dialogue goes something like this: *What gives me the right to stand in front of all these people and talk? What if they think I'm a fraud? There are smarter people than me around, so what makes me such an expert?*

We all suffer from 'imposter syndrome', especially at first. It strikes fear into speakers everywhere and it's what keeps most people sitting in the audience rather than standing at the lectern. You never really overcome it, but you do learn to accept it. You need to remember a couple of things.

First, there is only one you! You are the only person who has had your individual set of experiences, so by speaking from the heart you are conveying something original.

Second, you don't need to know more than everyone in your industry. You just need to be able to share a few new insights with the audience you are talking to.

Using the web to enhance speaking engagements

There are some very effective ways to leverage your engagement as a conference speaker. Let's look at the things you can do before, during and after your presentation.

In the lead-up to the event

- Check out who else is speaking and connect with the interesting ones on LinkedIn.

- Follow the Twitter hashtag, and connect with people who will be attending.

- If you find attendees who might make a great case study, connect with them and ask if you can mention them. This shows you've really done your homework and know your audience.

- Include your Twitter handle and conference hashtag on your slides.

- Upload your slide to Slideshare and set up a resources page for attendees to access your slides and any other links, tools or videos that might be useful.

- Meet and chat with a few attendees before you speak.

During your presentation

- In addition to delivering a knockout presentation, explain to your audience that while many MCs will ask them to turn off their phones, you'd like them on so they can tweet about the talk in real time. Tell them your Twitter handle and event hashtag.

- Try offering a prize for the best tweet, as judged by you, when you review the tweets once you're off stage.

- Schedule tweets during your talk. Use a tweet scheduling tool like Buffer or HootSuite to publish tweets (with the event hashtag) that coincide with important points you are making in your talk. To the audience it will seem like magic that you are tweeting while speaking on stage!

- Mention the resources page you have set up, and get them to write it down if they are interested.

- Make it easy for people who wish to opt-in to your email newsletter by collecting their business cards. We offer to email attendees all our free resources.

- Business-card draws are another fun way to increase audience participation.

- Always give attendees the choice of whether they want to opt-in to your newsletter or just the business-card draw. (We ask them to put a line through their email address if they don't want us to email them.)

Pro Tip: Film your presentation.

It is common for the event organiser to have a camera person film the speakers. If they haven't set this up, ask if you can bring along a friend or camera person yourself. It's good practice to watch your presentations so you can improve next time, and if it's a good presentation and well filmed, you can turn it into a highlights reel for YouTube.

After the presentation

- Try a transcription service like Shoeboxed to siphon all the business card information into a spreadsheet. Or photograph the cards and have a virtual assistant transcribe them for you.

- If you've collected people's business cards, make sure you email them with the promised resources as soon as you can.

- Connect with people you've met on LinkedIn.

- Ask a few people for LinkedIn endorsements.

- Send the conference organiser a thank-you card or small gift.

Summary

→ The secret to online is offline.

→ The real value of conferences lies in the people you meet and the connections you make.

→ Attend events and connect with aspirational contacts and other attendees.

→ Running your own events has risks, but it's also a great opportunity.

→ Consider public speaking as a way to build your community and attract leads.

Tools and templates

Event Marketing Template
www.bluewiremedia.com.au/event-marketing-template

Speakers Social Media Template
www.bluewiremedia.com.au/speakers-social-media-template

Buffer
www.bufferapp.com

Elance
www.elance.com

Eventbrite
www.eventbrite.com

HootSuite
www.hootsuite.com

Logitech pointers
We prefer the Logitech 2.4GHz Cordless Laserpointer Presenter ($299), but the Logitech Professional Presenter R800 ($80) is a good entry option.

oDesk
www.odesk.com

Shoeboxed
www.shoeboxed.com.au

PayPal
www.paypal.com

Confessions of a Public Speaker by Scott Berkun

Chapter 15

How to sell online while keeping your integrity

Teaching sells.

Brian Clark

Some time after Adam had bought, read and implemented the advice in Glenn Murray's *SEO Secrets* (discussed in chapter 12), he discovered something strange: he actually had two copies of the e-book on his computer, and the first copy long pre-dated his purchase. Yep, he already owned a copy of the e-book, and had done for 18 months. When he traced it back, he found that it had been forwarded to him for free by a friend, but he hadn't read it, let alone put it into action.

So which gave better value—the free copy or the one he paid $79 of his hard-earned money for? The paid one, of course!

Charging a fee is often in your customer's best interest

The realisation that came crashing home was that paying for something gives it intrinsic value. Since you value it more, you are much more likely to take action. The value Adam got from Glenn's book was many times what he paid for it. The copy of the same book that he'd received for free had precisely zero value—because he didn't even open it!

It seems logical that giving things away for free to your customer is better value to them than paying, until you consider the *SEO Secrets* story. While it appears counter-intuitive, if your goal is to deliver maximum value then in many cases you are best off charging your customer. There's something about pulling out your credit card and paying money that commits you to action.

Overcoming our fear of selling online

It's common to feel uncomfortable when you first start selling online. We certainly felt vulnerable making our first commercial offer via email, because we were stepping out from the safety of our free newsletter and exposing ourselves to the possibility of rejection. However, if you value your time and the results you want your customers to enjoy, it's important to become comfortable with the idea of selling online. We always remind ourselves of the following: we have offered plenty of our best thinking for free through blogs, podcasts, webinars, videos, emails and downloadable tools, but there are people who want to dive deeper into web marketing, and are willing to pay for it. So we viewed it as a moral obligation to provide the products and services that met these people's needs.

What to sell?

You can sell just about anything on the web these days, and most buyers are accustomed to being only a click away from a purchase. This means the opportunities are huge, and all you need is a PayPal account to get started.

We've found that a great place to start is to translate your existing products or services into something accessible via the web. For example, selling tickets to an event is made easy with Eventbrite. Packaging your IP into an e-book and selling it via E-junkie is also very easy, and you can sell your e-book on Kindle too. You can set up a membership site where people pay a monthly subscription fee to access your content, such as premium videos, tutorials and live webinars. Physical products can be sold through Amazon. If you sell consulting services, you can open yourself up to a global audience by offering consultations via Skype.

Start by selling someone else's product as an affiliate

Even if you haven't created any products yet, you can sell someone else's as an affiliate and earn a decent commission for yourself. After successfully implementing Glenn Murray's *SEO Secrets* e-book, we decided to join his affiliate program, where we could earn a 50 per cent commission on any sales we helped generate. It was all tracked by software that measured the clicks from our unique affiliate URL. We would write a genuine review of the e-book on our blog, tweet about it and share our experience with our email subscribers, and we would direct readers to a call-to-action to buy the e-book if they were interested. We sold plenty of Glenn's e-books and, more importantly for us, got the itch to sell our own products.

Only promote products you truly believe in. They should be products you have used yourself or have been created by people you trust — ideally both.

Most people with a digital product will have an affiliate program.

If you are looking for an affiliate product to start selling, you can always try our Web Marketing That Works online course.

Creating our own products

After the thrill of seeing commissions coming into our PayPal account, we decided it was time to package our own IP into a product. We opted to release everything we used in private web strategy consultations with clients, and packaged up 14 documents in our DIY Web Strategy Toolkit, which included the workbook, facilitator's guide, agendas, tools, resources and examples. We made this available for instant download on our website for $247. We did a soft launch on social media, and once our first sale had been processed smoothly, we pulled the trigger on our email launch.

It was our first digital product launch to our subscriber list, which was then roughly 3000 strong, and it earned us just under $3000 in sales at launch. Now that isn't huge numbers by product launch standards, but it validated the concept and proved that our readers were prepared to buy from us online. Since then we've launched other products, courses and events and earned over six figures in online sales.

How to sell online without selling your soul

As a content marketer, you're going to be selling something online eventually. We're in business, after all, so it's important to make sales, win customers and increase revenue.

Here are some tips to keep in mind:

- *First, forget social media.* For selling, social media is going to disappoint you. Social media is *social*—that is, it allows you to personalise your business and chat among your friends and prospective customers. It's great for nurturing relationships, building trust and growing your audience. All these are definitely important but it won't drive sales. It's not the right platform. Just like trying to close a business deal at a birthday party, it's nearly always inappropriate. You want to close deals in a business setting, which is email.

- *Email marketing is where the action is.* When it comes to making sales, email is at least 20 times more effective than Twitter, Facebook and LinkedIn combined, provided you have a strong email subscriber base that trusts you. But the big question that remains is how do you sell online without alienating your audience? Here's how.

- *Keep your voice consistent.* Your community of followers will be familiar with your tone of voice and personality. If you suddenly go from Friendly Trusted Adviser to Obnoxious Salesperson, you'll lose your audience in droves. Unfortunately, too many people suffer from a personality transplant when it comes to selling on the web. They start pressuring potential customers with hard-sell techniques. Lots of CAPITALS, exclamation marks, hype-filled headlines, yellow highlighter and red font. The transformation is off-putting.

- *Remember, you'll be back.* You can understand why some people become pushy when they sell. Historically, marketers have had only one chance to close (think infomercials and advertorials), so they crank up the pressure to buy and make you feel guilty or ashamed if you don't. They'll never see you again, so they don't care. But you're in a different boat. You have a *relationship* with your audience, and you'll be back next week, next month and next year, so you know how important this is.

- *Be yourself.* A good offer, urgency, bonuses and honest promises are certainly critical to a successful online sale, but you don't need to be pushy. Follow the same principles, but just be yourself. Definitely explain the value, tell us how long your offer lasts and the reasons why we should buy, share your testimonials and your guarantee, but do it like you're telling your best friend, not a stranger you'll never see again.

- *Be generous and people will want to buy.* To succeed online, you *genuinely* need to put the interests of your audience ahead of your own agenda. To sell before you've established trust is a damaging exercise. People who feel violated or manipulated won't ever be back.

---

*The key is **generosity**. Once you've built up trust, people will want to buy from you.*

- *Provide value.* Remember, when you're selling it's really not very different from your usual communications, except your customer is giving you their *money* as well as their attention. You need to deliver significantly more value when you want people to type in their credit card number.

- *Provide a phone number.* If you show people how they can get in contact with you, it helps reassure them about their purchase.

How to write a sales email

For starters, it is worth restating that the more trust your audience has in you, the more they will buy. It becomes less about sales techniques in the email and more about the relationship you have with the reader.

Here are the main components in an effective sales email. The key here is to understand the principles and how to apply them, and then to flavour the message with your own personality.

Text-only emails

As we discussed earlier, text-only emails have worked best for us when selling. It's best if it comes from one person as opposed to a company, and is worded as if it is written to one person.

An email sales letter needs to apply some of the same techniques as direct-response copywriting, such as having a single, clear call-to-action and a compelling value proposition. However, the key is to do it in a soft-sell way that appeals to those who are ready to buy and doesn't repel the rest of your readers.

You'll be back next week, and you want your readers to be there too, so don't pressure or cajole them.

We've actually found a short sales email performs twice as well as a long one.

The reason for a sales email is to direct readers to take the next step, which is to visit the sales web page.

'From name' and subject lines

Keeping the subject line short and the 'from name' personal has worked best for us. Again, write the subject as if you were writing to one person.

Email copy

Highlight the pain points that the reader may be facing and explain how your product may solve these. Invite the reader to take you up on your offer by clicking through to find out more or to buy. Demonstrate the value of your offer and then reveal your price. Offering bonuses effectively bolsters your value proposition too.

Letting readers know when the offer expires or how many items are left introduces scarcity and urgency, which also helps drive action. It's also wise to offer guarantees to reduce the risk for the buyer. Sign off the email as you would normally and then finish with a P.S. Postscripts are very effective because they're the last thing people read, so it's good to reiterate your call-to-action here.

Pro Tip: Use the word 'because'.

Simply using 'because' and then explaining the reason why you are making your offer is proven to help sales.

Here's a sample template you can edit. Download the Email Sales Copy Template from www.bluewiremedia.com.au/email-sales-copy-template.

From: Adam Franklin
Subject: Course offer

Hi Sam,

How are you?

If you've got ambitious marketing goals and you're not entirely sure how you'll achieve them, perhaps we can help.

As you know, Toby and I are committed to giving away most of our IP for free to help you with your web marketing, but we reserve our very best stuff, where the 10X value lies, for people who are ready to take action.

I'm writing to you today because I thought you might like to enrol/ buy/register for _____ and get all the bonuses too.

From now until _____, you can access it for the special price of $_____. Only X opportunities are available, so please be quick and <u>click here if you're interested</u>.

If you've got any questions, please hit reply or call me on 1300 258 394.

Cheers,
Adam

P.S. As always, our products come with a money-back guarantee, no questions asked. <u>Check it out</u> and Toby and I look forward to working with you.

Pro Tip: Send a short follow-up email.

In your initial offer, many readers will click the link in your email but not buy immediately. These are the people who are considering your offer and who may need a gentle reminder. Send them a short follow-up email 24 hours before the offer expires. This reminder email has always driven lots of extra sales.

For example:

> *From: Adam Franklin*
> *Subject: Can I help?*
>
> *Hi Sam,*
>
> *If you're still deciding about _____, please let me know how I can help. Simply reply or call me on 1300 258 394. Just a friendly reminder that the offer expires tomorrow.*
>
> *Thanks,*
> *Adam*
>
> *P.S. Here's that link when you're ready.*

Anatomy of an effective sales page

Sales web pages incorporate the elements of an effective landing page *and* compelling sales copy.

Remember the key elements of landing pages that apply are as follows:

- No main navigation (or other 'leaks').
- Social proof (such as number of customer or social media shares).
- Testimonials.
- Guarantees.
- A 3D icon or product image.
- A clear call-to-action to buy.
- Assurances that the payments facilities are secure.

The key elements of sales copy are as follows:

- Identify the pain point.
- Present the solution to the pain.
- Demonstrate value.

- Explain the benefits.

- Offer bonuses.

- Provide testimonials and endorsements.

- Invite the reader to imagine their life in the future when their problem has been solved.

- Provide a guarantee (risk reversal).

- Include a clear call-to-action.

Summary

→ Charging your customers can be in their best interest.

→ Trust is by far the most important element when it comes to selling online.

→ Email works best for selling online, and there are some basic tested techniques you can follow.

Tools and templates

Email Sales Copy Template
www.bluewiremedia.com.au/email-sales-copy-template

Become an affiliate with Bluewire Media
www.bluewiremedia.com.au/affiliate-program

E-junkie
www.e-junkie.com

Eventbrite
www.eventbrite.com

PayPal
www.paypal.com

SEO Secrets by Glenn Murray
http://bluewi.re/SEO-Secrets-e-book

Part VI

Social media

Chapter 16

Social media in action: strategy and guidelines

Content is fire, and social media is the gasoline.

Jay Baer

Social media is a real polariser of the marketing and business world. Many still dismiss it as a waste of time, and many more struggle to reap the potential rewards. There are a lot of mixed feelings about it because it is so new, incredibly diverse and constantly changing. But while there are horror stories and success stories in equal measure, most people simply want to see the value for their own company.

The pub and the dinner party of the internet

We like to knock off after a week of work to socialise, go to dinner parties and shoot the breeze with friends. Socialising can strengthen relationships, open doors, help close deals and be a lot of fun. So can social media.

Unless you're Paris Hilton, socialising isn't a stand-alone business or career path. It doesn't work on its own. It's the icing on the cake, but you need the cake first. Once the foundation of web marketing is laid, *then* the huge opportunity of social media comes into play.

The final pillar in your web marketing strategy

We've deliberately left the social media focus until last in this book, not because it's least important, but because it should come last in your marketing strategy. Commercial relationships can be strengthened and new relationships formed *socially* (on and offline), but this isn't a substitute for the actual 'commerce' that needs to occur in order to run or market a business.

When you have the foundation in place, social media can amplify your efforts and see your results explode.

The way some experts talk it up, though, you'd think you could sit on Facebook all day and make money. And you can, *if* you have the system in place (website, landing pages, sales pages, products, email marketing and so on) and you're using social media to interact with customers and attract prospects into the sales funnel — but not without that foundation.

Most people use social media as a hobby. They keep in touch with friends, exchange tweets and post photos. Only a very small percentage of us (mainly marketers and business owners) actually have the need and desire to implement a commercial framework.

Corporate executives sometimes have preconceived ideas about social media based on their own experience of teenagers spending hours glued to their smartphone and having fun with their friends. That worldview is understandable when it's all you've experienced. You have to see its potential and power with your own eyes to 'get it'.

The power of 'trust' over 'sell'

If you went to a business function and pestered everyone there with a sales pitch and your business card, you'd be sorely disappointed with your ROI. If you went along and met a few interesting people, had a chat, kept in touch, did generous things for them without expecting anything in return and continued this for years, then you'd have the foundation for a strong business relationship. It's the same deal with social media.

When it comes time to 'sell', a few people will respond to the call-to-action in your Facebook or Twitter update, but it's not really the place for it. You'll get a much better result from a well-crafted email, or a face-to-face meeting, particularly if it's a more complex sale.

Most people (about 90 per cent) trust recommendations by friends, but only 14 per cent trust ads. For us the aha! moment was realising that six times as many people would trust our message if they heard it from a friend rather than from us. That is powerful.

With so many options, where should you start?

Start by recalling the old adage 'You have two ears and one mouth. Use them in that order and ratio'. When in doubt, listen. Search Twitter for your company name and your own name, and listen to what people are saying. Do the same on the different social media platforms and get a baseline picture of what's happening. Of course, knowing what people are actually saying about you or your business can be confronting, but at least you know and can respond appropriately.

If someone is talking about you, what would you *like* them to be saying? This will help you craft how you want to be perceived. Take the time to think about how to interact with people who are saying good, bad or indifferent things about your company.

Take it one step further and search for keywords on Twitter, HootSuite and Social Mention. If you sell bikes in Sydney, plug those words in and listen. Now go ahead and secure your company name, and ideally your own name, on the major platforms like Facebook, Twitter, LinkedIn and Google+. Get in quick because you don't want to be too late, as Adam was when he had to settle for the back-to-front @Franklin_Adam Twitter handle.

Great. Next step—which platform is for me?

The section of the newspaper you flick to first may serve as a rough guide (thanks to our colleague Selina Power for this analogy). If you think of the different social media as the different sections of the newspaper, then:

- LinkedIn is the business and careers section.
- Blogging is the editorial.
- Blog comments are letters to the editor.
- Twitter is the headlines.
- Facebook is the social pages.
- Pinterest and Instagram are the lifestyle lift-outs.

- YouTube is the TV Guide.
- Google+ is the articles authored by credited journalists.

> ### Pro Tip: Use Google+ and Google Authorship.
>
> Building an audience and being active on Google+ positively impacts your Google rankings. Google Authorship means Google knows that you are the creator of a piece of content, regardless of where it is published online. This boosts your authority.

What is the ROI of social media?

This is usually the elephant in the room. It's also the question we all want answered, and thankfully it's a lot simpler than you'd think. There are three ways to answer it.

1. Ask how customers found you and work it out

The best way to determine your ROI is to trace how your customers found you in the first place and see what these people have spent. The most direct way is simply to ask your customers in person or on the phone. If you ask early enough in their journey with you, many customers will be able to tell you, so just make a note of it: 'Oh, I watched your YouTube video.' 'I read your blog.' 'I saw a tweet.'

Get a list of the customers who discovered you via social media. Add up how much they have spent with you and divide the total by what you've invested in social media. The simplest way is usually the best.

If you're more scientific in your approach, you can use paid software to track how a customer found your organisation and how they've interacted with you since. We use inbound marketing software Hubspot for this.

2. What is the ROI of using email or your telephone?

It's very hard to calculate the ROI, but they are communication tools without which your business could not run. Social media is fast becoming a critical communication tool too. We cannot imagine the next five to ten years *not* revolving around relationships formed and strengthened via social media.

3. The same 'tool' can produce vastly different outcomes

Imagine if you give identical surfboards to three different people. The first person doesn't surf, so the surfboard sits unused in their garage. No time or money invested.

The next surfboard you give to Toby. As a keen surfer, he would go ahead and buy a leg rope, wax, a board bag and a wetsuit to go with it, and probably book a surfing holiday. He'd spend time and money.

The third surfboard you give to Kelly Slater. He takes it and wins a surfing competition, and as world champion makes millions of dollars.

Exactly the same 'tool', vastly different outcomes.

Some people don't use social media at all and are missing out on the whole experience. But for most people social media is purely a hobby. They socialise on Facebook, read the news on Twitter and watch YouTube for recreation. And a small percentage of marketing and business professionals like us will be able to use the tools at our disposal to attract an audience, win customers and earn revenue.

Your social media strategy

To navigate social media successfully you first need a strategy. Here's a simple, step-by-step plan of attack to get your social media strategy in place.

1. Tactics and strategy

Strategically, what remarkable content will you publish? Keep your ideal customer in mind and create content that is specifically directed towards solving their problems. This way you'll earn your readers' trust and they'll be more likely to share your content and recommend you.

Tactically, you must decide which social networks you want to use, according to what will best suit the needs of your ideal customer. You'll likely choose among Facebook, Twitter, YouTube, LinkedIn, Google+ and new, fast-growing platforms such as Pinterest and Instagram.

2. Watching

Social media operates in real time, so you need an internal champion who watches and listens to what is being said on the web about your organisation. There are good free monitoring tools like Social Mention and HootSuite, and you can access these from a smartphone so your finger is always on the pulse.

3. Emergencies

What happens in the case of an emergency—a negative comment or a crisis?

Unless a negative comment is malicious or offensive, we strongly advise against deleting it. Certainly respond to the comment and offer your side of the story, but deleting the comment will simply throw fuel on the fire. Remember, having a few negative comments along with your sincere responses shows you are only human, and you may even be seen as more trustworthy as a result.

In a crisis situation, such as a scandal in the press, you need to know who will respond and represent the company. This should have been decided upon long before any crisis hits. Hopefully it never happens, but you should be prepared.

4. Employees

Decide who in your organisation, and which suppliers, will have access to your social media accounts and who is allowed to comment on your behalf.

Make sure you set clear expectations with your team to make the most of your social media activity.

Establishing legal social media policies and social media usage guidelines is important.

You can use our Social Media Guidelines Template as a starting point: www.bluewiremedia.com.au/free-social-media-guidelines-template. See the sample unrestricted version of the Social Media Guidelines Template at the end of this chapter.

5. Technology

Once you've decided which social media platforms you're planning to use, set up a profile in each, even if it's just to reserve your page and custom URL (such as www.facebook.com/BluewireMedia). There may be a company overseas with the same name as yours, so you'll want to be first in to reserve it.

6. Success

It's important to define why you're getting involved in social media in the first place. Keep your business objectives in mind and don't get obsessed with vanity metrics like numbers of followers, fans or likes. It's better to have a small audience of interested potential buyers than a huge but uninterested following.

Track who in your social media community goes on to become paying customers. Since you're running a business, it's great to know that you're getting an actual return on your time and money.

7. Content publishing schedule

Getting your social media strategy right before you start will help provide your framework moving forward, and ensure you stay focused on publishing great content for your buyer persona.

Those who get the best results with social media plan out what they'll be publishing and how frequently, and then have a system for holding themselves accountable for producing and sharing their content.

The only secrets to being successful in the social media space are practice and discipline.

Keep practising creating content and the quality will improve over time.

Then just keep the discipline going to do it regularly.

Most people who say social media doesn't work give up way too soon. Be persistent. The opportunities are huge.

To help you plan your activity, download the Social Media Planning Template from www.bluewiremedia.com.au/social-media-planning-template.

Establishing a risk management plan

'He's been taken in for questioning by the police.' This was the outcome of a comment on Facebook that had been posted less than 24 hours before. A straightforward Facebook update generated a string of friendly banter—until one, very nasty comment. It was violent and sexually explicit.

The comment was immediately screenshot then hidden, the user was blocked and the issue escalated to the relevant parties. They notified the police, who responded accordingly.

No one can foresee all possible scenarios. This was a 1 in 10 000 occurrence, but we were prepared for it. We had put in place a risk management plan including a five-level complaint grading system, with appropriate responses and processes mapped out for each level. It was crystal clear what needed to happen when the comment was posted.

It's sad that the process is required at all, but the potential for damage in social media comes from the unknowable scenario, the wild card, not just your regular complaints or what you've dealt with in the past.

There are two key factors here:

1   Someone was monitoring the page and saw the comment.

2   A plan was in place and it was followed.

It's time to set this up for you.

Watching

If you're the marketing manager or business owner, the important thing is that the responsibility for monitoring and responding is clearly assigned to a specific person. It may be you, or it may be the team member who is most comfortable with social media platforms and the appropriate tool. Remember to be clear about who will be in charge after hours, too.

There are plenty of tools available. The main thing is to ensure you have someone watching. We use a combination of HootSuite, Social Mention, and Hubspot to monitor our social media. We also use Google Alerts to keep track of our web mentions.

Responding to emergencies

No one likes to think there'll be an emergency, and fingers crossed there won't be. So face up to the risks, however small they may be.

In the example of a simple risk management strategy outlined in table 16.1, the marketing manager has the main monitoring responsibility.

Table 16.1: simple risk management strategy

What	Who	Process
Negative comment: Customer complaint	Marketing manager	Responds publicly to the complaint and requests complainant's contact details to discuss possible remedies offline.
		Makes a record of the complaint and response (screenshot).
Crisis: Rogue employee gets access to social media and makes defamatory statements	Marketing manager, CEO, legal adviser	Marketing manager announces that the company will comment shortly, takes a screenshot of the post(s), and advises the CEO and legal adviser. CEO responds once legal advice has been given.

A few reminders:

1 Sometimes the worst thing you can do is ignore a negative comment.

2 It is best always to respond in the medium in which the complaint arises. This way there is a public record that you care and have initiated action.

3 Maintaining 'house rules' on your social media profiles will help set expectations in your community on response times, what is and isn't acceptable, and potential consequences.

4 *Always* document complaints and responses.

5 If a comment breaches your house rules (say, because it is malicious or defamatory), you are entitled to remove it. However, *always* screenshot the comment before you delete it. Depending on the situation, it also may be appropriate to notify your community that it has been deleted and why.

Preparing your staff

Deciding what your team can and can't say and do on social media is another important step to managing the risks and maximising the opportunities of social media.

You can take an open stance that everyone can use it, or you can close your organisation right down. While we're not fans of the latter response, the most important aspect is to make a conscious decision and let your team know. If you decide to leverage social media to its maximum through your team, then training is a very good idea too.

Authority and technology

Make sure you determine who can use which platforms and who can speak on behalf of the company. This clarity upfront will help prevent issues arising when you get started building your community online.

You want to avoid the situation where different people in the company each set up company pages oblivious to the others. Dealing with and trying to consolidate a mess of disjointed pages is a nightmare.

Get your vanity URLs locked in for each of the platforms. Make sure you have the appropriate administrator access and all of the usernames and passwords kept securely.

Knowing what happens to your social media profiles when your authorised staff move on is a big part of reducing the risk.

Legal aspects

It's also important to understand that with a legal framework for your organisation it's much easier to train your colleagues and staff so they know how best to use social media.

It's always advisable to get lawyers to draft a legally binding policy. While social media guidelines are *not* legally binding, they are a great starting point. You can choose to use a conservative, moderate or unrestricted version.

Download our simple, editable Social Media Guidelines Template from www.bluewiremedia.com.au/free-social-media-guidelines-template. Check out the unrestricted version of the guidelines at the end of this chapter.

The green light

Understanding social media is one thing, but putting it into action is another entirely. Over the past few years, more and more company executives have invited us to come and speak to them about social media. Marketing managers are pushing for social media to be given the green light internally. If you are facing this situation, we encourage you to show the video 'Social Media Revolution' by Socialnomics on YouTube (www.youtube.com/user/Socialnomics09).

With the green light from above, and the appropriate social media guidelines and social media strategy in place, you can really begin to prove what's possible.

> *As you build your web marketing assets, you can really amplify your efforts with social media.*

Remember, though, that the foundation must be laid or you will fail to gain traction.

Beware the traps: vanity metrics

People often enter into social media with the aim of building a community on Twitter and Facebook and this is valuable, but keep your buyer personas in mind at all times. Getting lots of likes and followers feels good but, for your business, they need to be the right types of people, who may actually become customers.

It's easy to be distracted by chasing numbers for numbers' sake, so remember to stay focused on your business goals.

Listen up and save thousands on focus groups

Many companies won't hesitate to pay thousands of dollars on focus groups, yet all this data is now available for free, unfiltered and in real time. You don't need fancy software to give you positive and negative sentiment—just take a look at the raw data.

Pro Tip: Print it out.

Print out what people are really saying about your company, and take that to your management meetings. Oscar Wilde said: 'The only thing worse than being talked about is not being talked about.' If you can't find anything to print, that's a compelling reason to ask why.

Getting active on social media

Once you've listened in on the conversations, built a strategy and developed your social media guidelines, then you need to get that content rhythm going.

Adam's social media calendar looks like this:

Monday morning (30 minutes)

- Scan blog feed on Feedly for interesting articles.

- Comment on the best articles.

- Share the best posts on social media by scheduling with Buffer.

- Mix in a handful of our free tools and e-books, and our own blog posts.

Monday afternoon (2 to 3 hours)

- Write the Bluewire News email and schedule it for Wednesday, 6 am.

Wednesday morning (1 hour)

- Once the Bluewire News is sent out, add it to our website.

- Share it on Twitter, Facebook, LinkedIn and Google+.

- Reply to readers who write in.

Thursday afternoon (2 to 3 hours)

- Write a blog post or guest blog post.

- Spend 45 minutes promoting the blog post.

Saturday morning (30 minutes)

- Send the follow-up Bluewire News and reply to readers.

Out and about:

- Post a photo to Facebook or Instagram.

- Interview an interesting person to post to YouTube.

In dead time (waiting for a meeting, in transit and so on)

- Reply to @mentions on Twitter, comments on blog posts and LinkedIn discussions.

As you can see, this involves a commitment of about eight hours, but that includes creating a blog post and writing an email newsletter.

| Company LOGO | **Social media guidelines** |

XYZ Company is an organisation that actively embraces social media.

As a rule of thumb: be real and use your best judgement — we trust you!

- All staff are allowed and encouraged to blog and use Twitter, Facebook, Linked In, YouTube and Google+.

- If you use your own 'personal' persona for twitter (eg. @yourname) then of course you are free to keep that if you decide to leave.

- If you use an 'XYZ Company' persona (eg. @XYZ_Support) it's expected that you hand that account over if you decide to leave.

- Please provide usernames and passwords of 'XYZ Company' personas and agree not to change them without notification.

- If you make a 'mistake' please own up to it immediately, apologise and be genuine.

- When commenting as an individual, please use the 1st Person (eg. I, me, mine). Official announcements will be from @XYZ_Company.

- Please think before you tweet, blog or post a comment — remember what you say lives online forever!

- Do not use false or fake personas.

- Never reveal any confidential or proprietary information or make disparaging, offensive or spammy comments.

- Breach of this policy may result in dismissal, including if inappropriate comments are made regarding your employment via personal or XYZ Company personas and regardless of the time of day it occurs.

These guidelines will be regularly reviewed to ensure continued effectiveness and improvement.

Name
Managing Director (or relevant title)
XYZ Company
Date

Summary

→ Social media is the amplifier of your web marketing strategy.

→ Listen first. Monitor your social media to gain customer insights.

→ Put a plan in place to deal with negative comments and emergencies so you are prepared.

→ Train your team in how to use social media.

→ Choose the best platforms for your business and secure your social media profiles.

→ Make sure your social media metrics align with your business goals.

Tools and templates

Social Media Guidelines Checklist
www.bluewiremedia.com.au/free-social-media-guidelines-template

Social Media Planning Template
www.bluewiremedia.com.au/social-media-planning-template

Social Media Image Sizes Checklist
www.bluewiremedia.com.au/social-media-image-sizes-checklist

Buffer
www.bufferapp.com

HootSuite
www.hootsuite.com

Social Media Revolution video
www.youtube.com/user/Socialnomics09

Mention
www.mention.net

Chapter 17

LinkedIn: the essential social network for business

It's not about B2C [Business to Consumer] or B2B [Business to Business] anymore. It's about P2P [People to People].

Verne Harnish

LinkedIn is *the* social network for our business. If we had to sacrifice all other networks to stay with only one, LinkedIn is where we'd be. It has always been handy, even in its basic form, as the home of your online résumé and Rolodex (your business card file). In recent years it has become so much more than that. LinkedIn is now the go-to source for business news, a content publishing platform and a customer relationship manager (CRM).

Everything we discuss here is accessible using the free version of LinkedIn.

LinkedIn for beginners

Joining LinkedIn is very simple, requiring you to follow a few basic steps.

Set up your account

Either you have your LinkedIn profile set up or your email inbox is full of LinkedIn requests from friends trying to connect with you and urging you to join.

Accept connection requests

At its simplest, LinkedIn has replaced the old-school Rolodex, but it's better than that because it updates itself. Before LinkedIn, when the people in your network changed jobs and got a new email address you'd be left wondering how to reach them, unless of course you were close enough to have their mobile number.

Get your profile to 100 per cent

If you follow LinkedIn's prompts, you'll be well on your way to completing your profile. The first step is to add a recent photo of yourself. Then fill in your work history and education, list any publications you've released, and seek endorsements and recommendations from people you know. You'll look the part if you follow these steps, and you can add to your profile at any time.

Keep in mind that this isn't an exercise in vanity; it's about developing your digital footprint. Your LinkedIn profile is one of the first entries to appear in a Google search of your name and, like it or not, most people who are considering engaging you or working for you will take a look at this before they even contact you. It's that important.

> **Pro Tip: Add video and slides to your LinkedIn profile.**
>
> To really add pizazz to your profile, add a YouTube video and a Slideshare presentation.

Grow your network

Start growing your network each week by connecting with a handful of people via LinkedIn's 'people you might know' feature. If you haven't already done so, you'll be amazed to bump into old colleagues, school friends and perhaps people who you might like to do business with.

Privacy settings

What many people don't realise is that the default settings on LinkedIn allow other people to see when you've looked at someone's profile. Understandably, this can make people uncomfortable, and luckily there's an easy way to disable it.

If you value anonymity, this is a wise move. Log in, go into Accounts & Settings (in the top right corner) and review your Privacy & Settings. On the Profile tab, you can 'Edit your public profile'. This way you can navigate LinkedIn without people knowing your every click.

If you are hunting around for a job or client you may not want your new connections to be broadcast to your whole network. You can increase your privacy by changing the setting called 'Turn off/on your activity broadcasts', so any new connections, recommendations or companies you follow are not published.

> ## Pro Tip: LinkedIn Contacts is CRM gold.
>
> LinkedIn Contacts has excellent CRM features that allow you to tag contacts, add notes and reminders, and record how you met them. It really is an amazing free service and a huge help in managing your ever-growing network of business contacts.

LinkedIn Contacts will even sync with your Gmail account to let you know what meetings you have in your Calendar, and you'll see your email history with that person too. It is ideal for refreshing your memory prior to sales calls, meetings and events.

> ## LinkedIn marketing in 5 minutes a day — beginners
>
> - Respond to pending requests (1 minute).
> - Send a thank-you or hello note to new contacts (3 minutes).
> - Request one new contact out of LinkedIn's 'people you may know' feature (1 minute).

LinkedIn for intermediates

As a newbie, if you use LinkedIn as outlined here, you will pick it up quickly and see its enormous potential. Soon you'll be ready to move deeper.

> ### Pro Tip: Connect with people you don't know yet.
>
> Just like offline, be open to interacting with people you don't know yet. For example, as a speaker, Adam loves it when people in the audience connect with him before or after his presentation. It's a great way to keep in touch.

It's the place for business news.

LinkedIn's 'Pulse' is fast becoming the go-to place for business news. You can read unique articles written by a wide range of LinkedIn Influencers and well-known business leaders, such as Sir Richard Branson, Bill Gates, Arianna Huffington and Barack Obama, plus all the major business news outlets including *Forbes*, *Time*, *Fortune* and the *Wall Street Journal*.

It's a free content-sharing platform with an inbuilt audience.

Directing readers to a brand-new blog can be like pulling teeth, but with LinkedIn you can share blog updates with your entire professional network by posting content. Publishing your articles to LinkedIn Groups also helps you to introduce your content to new readers.

Be noticed by adding value to your network. Even if you don't publish your own blog yet, you can deliver value to your network by curating the best articles you read online and sharing them on LinkedIn. You'll be helping your connections find good content and when you're ready to write and post your own articles, you'll have a captive audience who trusts you.

LinkedIn for jobs and recruitment

As a job seeker, you can easily apply for jobs listed on LinkedIn, for free.

Similarly, companies can pay to post jobs on LinkedIn. Remember, the best people and the best employers rarely need to advertise. If you are proactive on LinkedIn you can become a known quantity and attract the best opportunities.

LinkedIn Company Pages

It's a good move to set up your Company Page on LinkedIn. It has a different set of benefits compared with using only your personal profile. For starters, your team can all be identified as employees, which is verified via their email address. Also, anyone on LinkedIn can follow your organisation, so you can grow your social network this way. Additionally, you can post your products and services to a Company Page and can view analytics.

However, one of the things we've found with LinkedIn is that people like to connect directly with people rather than companies—they prefer the human element.

Do you allow staff to build their own LinkedIn network?

In short, yes, of course you do. You encourage it and reward it! Why? Firstly, to dictate what people do with their own web networks is draconian (even though some employers still put it in their employment contract).

Secondly, it is in the best interest of business owners or marketing managers to enable their best asset—their people. Every person has contacts in their social networks. The power of enabling these networks, and having so many advocates on the 'digital frontline', is incredible. Your staff are the people serving your customers, and allowing them to use the best tools at their disposal is essential.

Now to address the cynics' concerns.

What if staff leave and steal my clients?

This is a business threat more than a social media threat. You allow staff an email address and a mobile phone, and it's part of many people's jobs to develop relationships with clients. So if staff move on, it doesn't take a client long to track them down, with or without social media, and you can't force clients to stay with you.

The goal should be to make your company so great that they want to stay with you.

What if they misrepresent the company?

If you don't trust them, move them on. For everyone else, you need to provide social media guidelines. If someone isn't sure how to use a social media platform, it's your responsibility as an employer to train them and provide the necessary framework so they know what is expected. People make mistakes. We're all guilty of that, but we learn from them. Of course, if staff do anything malicious or damaging (online or offline), then that can be a dismissible offence.

LinkedIn marketing in 5 minutes a day — intermediate

- See who has viewed your profile and reach out to the interesting ones (3 minutes).

- Share a piece of your content on your profile (2 minutes).

LinkedIn for advanced users

LinkedIn continues to increase its offerings as you discover new ways to use it. For sales, marketing and HR professionals it has well and truly changed the game. It is another great way to show your credibility, win clients, attract staff and propel your business.

Get proactive

Keep an eye on who has viewed your profile via LinkedIn's inbuilt feature. It's nice to know that people are taking an interest in you, so treat them as you would in real life. Say hello, reach out to thank them and see how you might be able to help.

Remember, the key always is to lead with generosity and not to expect anything in return.

This habit alone can lead to many interesting encounters and fun connections.

Get your content published on LinkedIn Pulse

You have the opportunity to submit your own blog articles to LinkedIn for publication on Pulse alongside news and posts from the Influencers. To be considered you must have the inShare plug-in (the LinkedIn Share button) so members can share the article. You must also have a LinkedIn Company Page. Once you meet these two basic criteria you can submit your site at www.pulse.me/publishers and also contact publisher@linkedin.com to ask any further questions.

Advanced search

The 'advanced search' feature on LinkedIn is another gold mine that you can use to find ideal clients, staff or aspirational contacts. For example, our company's typical private client is a 'marketing manager in Sydney', so we can search under the keyword phrase 'marketing manager' for someone currently in the role and within a 15 km radius of the postcode 2000.

This is very powerful. Knowing who is who at organisations used to take a lot of research, and it required personal introductions to connect with them. LinkedIn solves this problem.

Just because you know who they are, however, doesn't mean you barge on in and harass them with sales pitches or meeting requests. If you physically walked into a room full of your ideal customers, you wouldn't spin round the room bugging them all, would you? We hope your answer is no. Instead you'd be polite, start conversations, ask questions and contribute to conversations.

> **Pro Tip: Join Groups your buyer personas are in.**
>
> Read all the discussions, identify their pain points and get to know the people in the groups. By commenting, joining discussions and helping people, you'll show up on their radar.

Connect with purpose

If you've identified someone you'd like to connect with, it's very easy to determine who you have in common through your first-, second-, and third-degree contacts. You can then know who to ask for an introduction.

Make sure your profile is up-to-date because that's the first thing they'll be looking at.

As always, the key is to lead with generosity and get to know these people by helping them first.

LinkedIn marketing in 5 minutes a day — advanced

- Submit an article to LinkedIn Pulse (2 minutes).

- Comment on an Influencer's article (3 minutes).

LinkedIn for genuine influencers

Dave Kerpen, author of *Likeable Business*, holds the mantle as LinkedIn's most trafficked influencer, ahead of folks like Barack Obama, Sir Richard Branson and Jack Welch. LinkedIn introduced its Influencer program in 2012, and has taken on a small but influential group of people to write regular posts. These individuals are a diverse mix of business leaders, celebrities, presidents, marketers and many others. Dave has had over 2.4 million views of his articles, and this has led to $1 million in direct business and a network of people Dave can now call friends.

This success demonstrates that blogging has truly reached critical mass. Unfortunately for us mere mortals, the Influencer program has a waiting list of over 50 000 applicants, and in our interview for this book, Kerpen (only half) joked that now they were pretty much only accepting heads of state and Fortune 500 CEOs!

Nevertheless, LinkedIn is the platform that has something for everyone in a professional sense. Get started today if you haven't yet. Who knows, one day you may be rubbing shoulders with Obama, Branson and Dave Kerpen.

We'd love to connect with you on LinkedIn. Please mention the book so we know you're a reader:

Adam Franklin: au.linkedin.com/in/adamfranklin

Toby Jenkins: au.linkedin.com/in/tobyjenkins

Summary

→ Complete your profile and review your privacy settings.

→ Connect with people and share content.

→ Train your team to use it well.

→ Join Groups and proactively network.

→ Submit your articles to LinkedIn Pulse for greater exposure opportunities.

Tools and templates

LinkedIn Share button
http://developer.linkedin.com/plugins/share-plugin-generator

LinkedIn Pulse submission
www.pulse.me/publishers/ and also contact publisher@linkedin.com

How to set up a Company Page
http://marketing.linkedin.com/company-pages

LinkedIn 5 min Marketing Plan
www.bluewiremedia.com.au/linkedin-daily-marketing-plan

Chapter 18

Facebook: a gold mine for marketers

Nothing influences people more than a recommendation from a trusted friend.

Mark Zuckerberg

Facebook has saved Bluewire Media tens of thousands in recruitment costs. Before Facebook there was one situation where we had to pay more than $13 000 in fees when we needed to grow our team. For a small business, that was a hit we didn't enjoy. Then Facebook burst onto the scene. Fast-forward four years and our Facebook page served as our recruitment tool. Not only have we avoided paying recruiters obscene fees, but we've had a steady supply of applicants who already know us through Facebook.

Take our social media adviser, Selina Power, for example. Selina noticed everything Bluewire Media was doing on Facebook, Twitter and LinkedIn. We immediately earned her approval for being active on the major social media platforms. So Selina followed our Facebook page. She saw that we were having conversations with people and posting real photos of our team doing fun things. The movie nights and birthday cakes showed Sel the human side of our team, which further piqued her interest. We had photos of lunches, 'fun manager' nights, Christmas parties, events, and general frivolity in the office. Selina knew our office arrangement and loved the fact it was open plan (with no cubicles); she had even earmarked the desk area she wanted to occupy!

Facebook business page

For those who are new to Facebook, the way it works is that individuals can become 'fans' of an organisation's business page. Our business page was doing more for us than a team of recruiters could. Our team was all over the Bluewire Facebook page, and Selina simply wanted to join in.

So she took it upon herself to apply for an internship via our Facebook page link, and she offered her services as a social media intern for four weeks to prove her ability to run a hands-on social media offering. It was a no-risk proposition for us, so we took her on. We had an understanding that if she could drum up enough business to cover a wage and overheads, then we'd be in a position to lock in a new role.

As an employer, it's your dream to have highly talented, motivated and innovative people go out of their way to work with you. It sure beats interviewing multiple applicants who have given only a cursory glance to your website pre-interview, and then forking out $13 000 in recruitment fees.

> ## Pro Tip: Take your camera everywhere.
>
> Most smartphones have a great quality camera built into them. Be the person who takes the best photos at meet-ups, seminars and events. Get pics from around the office, ask your team to take photos at events they go to and get in the habit of posting them on Facebook. It's a great way to win new Facebook fans for your business page. People will tag photos and leave comments, and it's all happening on your Facebook page so people have a reason to 'like' you.

Facebook is a platform where you can make a real impact with people who are important to your company. Your fans will spend more time on Facebook than on your website, so it's good to be active and sharing your content there too.

Be consistent, present and active so you can leverage your broader marketing activities.

Getting more fans

How to get more fans? It's the million-dollar question, isn't it? We all want a Facebook page with plenty of active fans liking our photos, leaving comments and sharing our posts. There are several ways to achieve this.

Invite people in your existing community

One of the best ways to kick-start the growth of your Facebook page is to invite people you know personally to join, then ask people who receive your regular newsletter to 'like' you. You can activate your Twitter, LinkedIn and Google+ audiences to become fans on Facebook too. Those who already know you are most likely to lead the charge to your Facebook page.

Facebook Like Box

Another great way to leverage your existing web traffic is to install the free Like Box on your blog. Google 'Facebook WordPress Like Box' to upload the plug-in. Or, if you're running a non-WordPress website, go to the Facebook developers' site at https://developers.facebook.com/docs/reference/plugins/like-box.

When people visit your site they will see which of their friends already like your page. This provides social proof that your page is popular. Yes, Facebook is a key part of your web marketing; nevertheless you should never make your 'like' call-to-action more prominent on your blog or website than your email opt-in.

Our suggestion is that you attract email subscribers first and aim to get them onboard as Facebook fans next.

Attracting fans and getting likes on your page is the obvious metric because it's so conspicuous on your page. It's an open question whether we'd all be so obsessed about it if that number was less public.

Some ways to get noticed — or passed over

It pays to know the things that help and hinder your chances of getting seen.

For example, to help your visibility:

- *Tell fans exactly what you want them to do, using Facebook language.* Use a clear call-to-action — for example, 'Like this post' or 'Share this post with your friends'. Share is the best verb to use because it has the most influence on bringing visibility to your posts.

- *Write for your fans' friends.* Every time you write a Facebook update that your fans want to share with their friends, you increase your reach. And your message will be six times more trustworthy because people receive it directly from a friend rather than from a company. This should be your primary focus when growing your organic fan base.

- *Ask one question at a time.* Otherwise you will confuse fans, which leads to inaction rather than action.

- *Try yes/no questions.* Sometimes you'll find that asking a closed (yes or no) question on Facebook makes it easier for fans to comment without thinking too much. This can raise the visibility of your post and any subsequent post. However, it can look like a stunt to maximise comments and fans will dodge it if they feel even slightly manipulated.

- *Upload a photo and add the URL in the description.* To get more likes, comments and shares, don't just add the URL and use the default thumbnail image, because you'll be missing an opportunity. Instead, uploading a photo and adding a URL in the description makes the photo much bigger and more likely that people will click and comment on it.

On the other hand, your chances of being seen will be reduced if:

- your page or post is reported as spam

- people hide your posts

- people select 'I don't want to see this'

- people un-like your page.

> ## Facebook marketing in 5 minutes a day
>
> - Check your notifications and respond appropriately (2 minutes).
> - Post a piece of content, such as a picture or question, to your Business Page (3 minutes).

Download Facebook 5 Minute Marketing Plan from www.bluewiremedia .com.au/facebook-marketing-plan.

Be careful what you ask for

Always ask yourself whether your post could attract comments that might embarrass your organisation. For example, we once posted the innocuous question, 'What was the last movie you watched?' and one guy left a comment with the name of an obviously pornographic movie. Unfortunately it attracted a bunch of likes too! Embarrassing, yes, and we brought it on ourselves. He may have answered with gospel truth, but *we* posed the question. Lesson learned.

> ### Pro Tip: Before you post, ask yourself the following questions:
>
> - Would you comment on this post yourself?
> - What does this say about your organisation?
> - Can you think of any negative comments this post might trigger?
> - Does the post feature images of competitors?
> - Does the post or image contravene Facebook's terms and conditions?
> - Are there any spelling or grammatical errors in the content or image captions?
>
> See the Social Media Corporate Approval Template for the spreadsheet we use. It's a free download: www.bluewiremedia.com .au/social-media-corporate-approval-template.

Our best Facebook updates

We continue to be amazed by what content gets traction on Facebook. A picture of Sam sitting on a Swiss ball in the office was one of our most popular posts as it sparked a conversation among our fans. We even had one comment, with a link to the Occupational Health & Safety website, arguing that it was Bluewire's duty of care to provide conventional chairs in the office!

Another time, Selina posted a photo wondering whether the veggies in her garden were shallots or spring onions. The debate that ensued was funny and enlightening. We also invited fans to suggest a name for our new printer and after plenty of likes the winning name was 'A3's a Crowd'.

Very often articles that get plenty of traction on the blog barely raise a ripple on Facebook. The platforms are totally different, with Facebook definitely the more *social* of the social media.

Pro Tip: Check Facebook Insights for your most popular content.

Check in daily to see what your most popular content was so you can publish more material your fans like. Facebook's free Insights service will give you valuable analytics on your reach, likes and engagement, as well as the best time of day to post.

Closing the gap on content promotion

The more positive interactions you have on your page, the more your content will appear in fans' news feeds. However, the percentage of content your fans see is dropping as the sheer volume of Facebook content increases.

You have the opportunity to pay Facebook to 'promote your post'. This will mean it is shown not only to your own fans but to their friends too, so you increase the visibility of the post. Of course you pay for the privilege every time. Our own approach has been to avoid this route and use Facebook to support our recruitment efforts.

Yes, you pay to reach your own fans

One gripe among marketers is the fact that Facebook is increasingly asking you to pay even to reach your own fans. Facebook offers many great free services for marketers. It lets you build a community, design your Facebook page and message fans, all at no cost. However, Facebook is itself a business and it's made the decision to charge page owners to reach a greater percentage of their fans.

Facebook rewards great content that is liked and shared. So there are a number of tactics you can use to boost your visibility without resorting to paying for promotion. The most popular is running a contest or competition.

Are contests and competitions worthwhile?

Competitions can be very effective ways to drive visibility and increase your fan base. You must be careful not to attract the wrong types of fans, though. If you offer prizes that are unrelated to your business, you may find you attract a whole bunch of people who are eager for the prize rather than genuinely interested in your organisation. The additional risk is that if you get the wrong sorts liking your page, once the competition is over, they may un-like or hide your updates. Both of these send Facebook negative signals about your page, resulting in your page appearing in fewer news feeds.

Now the good news.

It works—if you give away prizes that are related to your business and appeal to your buyer personas. Attracting more of these people is obviously beneficial, especially if you avoid the pure 'competition crowd'.

A good competition will also increase engagement on your page because lots more people are interacting with it. This increases the visibility of your next post, so you need to make it a good one. For example, you might put up a stellar piece of premium content because you know many more people will see it. Remember: always check Facebook's terms and conditions before launching a competition as the rules change frequently.

Facebook-sponsored links to promote your page or post

As we've stated throughout the book, our approach has been to focus on organic marketing and avoid paying for advertising. But paid ads can certainly generate results for you. The two aspects to consider are (a) buying sponsored links on the right of the page to increase the number of your fans (you can be very targeted here), and (b) promoting your posts so your followers can see them. Both can no doubt amplify your own promotional efforts, but be aware that you'll be reaching back into your pocket each time.

> ### Pro Tip: Encourage your Facebook fans to opt in to your email.
>
> You can use the plug-ins Woobox or Shortstack to add a form field for email address and a checkbox. This way you can promote your flagship and premium content and nurture Facebook fans to become email subscribers, which is a much more trusting relationship. This becomes even more important when you consider that on average no more than 40 per cent of your fans are logged into Facebook at any one time, and if they're not logged in they'll miss your content.

As Jay Baer says, 'For someone to click one button, once, is hardly a blood oath of loyalty to your organisation'! Moving fans over to email has always been the secondary aim of our Facebook page, after attracting talent.

Selling on Facebook

Facebook really isn't the right place to sell products. Yes, you may get some sales, but it's like selling your wares at a family barbecue, or selling products at a community sausage sizzle. It's possible, and many people do it, but for most businesses selling takes place over email and on websites, or, in the offline world, over the phone or in meetings.

If you are looking to sell on Facebook, however, there is a plug-in shopping cart called Ecwid that allows you to sell products right on your page. It's free if you're selling up to 10 products.

At Bluewire Media, we don't sell directly on Facebook, but instead we promote events and products and direct people to our website to perform the actual transactions.

A note on privacy

Whether you like it or not, many employers and clients will stalk you on Facebook before they engage you. This shouldn't strike fear into you, but it's worth taking a quick look at what shows up in your public profile. You can always go in and change your settings if you want greater privacy.

As two people who are a whisker either side of the GenX–GenY age border, we typically find that people who have grown up with technology (aka digital natives) are largely unconcerned about having their lives plastered all over Facebook for the world to see. Their attitude is, 'I've got nothing to hide, and it's how we share our lives with our friends'. Generally speaking, baby boomers are horrified by this and fret about posting anything from their private life.

Of course, either extreme has its drawbacks. If you have your privacy settings completely locked down or have literally no social media presence, an employer might assume you are a criminal or a spy. And if it looks like you haven't been sober in weeks, it may be held against you too. But on the whole there's not much to worry about if you have a normal, active social life and you choose to share it on Facebook. Most employers recognise the value of leading a balanced and interesting life, just as you will appreciate that your employer supports a fun, friendly working environment.

Summary

→ Facebook is a very social network.

→ You can showcase your personality and that of your company.

→ You can attract talent and see inside the walls of organisations you might like to work with.

→ You can build a fan base, and we recommend you nurture them towards an email relationship.

→ Competitions can be used to increase the visibility of posts.

→ Review your profile so you know what an outsider sees.

Tools and templates

Social Media Corporate Approval Template
www.bluewiremedia.com.au/social-media-corporate-approval-template

Facebook 5 Minute Marketing Plan
www.bluewiremedia.com.au/facebook-marketing-plan

Ecwid
www.ecwid.com

Shortstack
www.shortstack.com

Woobox
www.woobox.com

Facebook 'Like' Box:

Facebook WordPress Like Box
http://wordpress.org/plugins/facebook-like-box-widget

Facebook developers' site (for non-WordPress sites)
https://developers.facebook.com/docs/reference/plugins/like-box

Chapter 19

Twitter: a communication revolution

You can't shortcut relationships.

Scott Stratten

Off the back of a Twitter exchange, we'd just locked in a meeting with the CEO of Deloitte, a billion-dollar revenue company.

It began when we saw a tweet from our friend Anne Sorensen praising Deloitte's social media policy. Here she spoke of a CEO of a well-known international advisory firm who not only had embraced Twitter within his organisation, but was himself very active on the platform. This was exactly the story our clients needed to hear.

We retweeted Anne and sent congratulatory tweets to the Deloitte team. After a short Twitter exchange we switched to email. Finally we mustered the courage to try to connect directly with Deloitte's CEO, Giam Swiegers, whose email address we found in the publicly available social media policy document. We dropped him a brief email to say thanks for being a great case study for our clients and to link him to our blog post about his firm. He emailed us right back:

Happy to chat

Giam

Wow, what a generous offer, and we hadn't even asked. Adam wrote back to say he'd be down in Sydney the following week and would love to interview him, suggesting when he could pop in.

That will be interesting... Michelle please arrange.

Giam Swiegers

CEO Deloitte Australia

Of course, this points to Giam's generosity rather than anything we could do for him. Writing a blog post about a firm in no way guarantees a meeting with its CEO, but this incident does highlight the magic that *can* happen with social media.

Digital immigration: learning from the natives

What interested us about Deloitte was the internal program they ran in which they matched up 'digital natives' (people, typically 30 and under, who have grown up with new technology) with self-proclaimed 'digital dinosaurs'. Once the two are paired up, the dinosaur has a technology mentor to learn from, and once they graduate they become 'digital immigrants'.

When we interviewed Giam for this book, we found his views remained largely unchanged from that first discussion three years ago. In fact, his advocacy of social media had got even stronger: 'I have just become more convinced that social media has and will have a big impact on communications and therefore on business and leaders. As a result we have increased our investment in social media training.'

His advice for fellow CEOs: 'Start using it as soon as possible. Twitter is a wonderful tool for incoming news. Use it for that to start off with and see how others use it. Find the way you are most comfortable with, but don't overuse it.'

Twitter is a game changer in opening up the possibility of following the conversations of all sorts of people and interacting with them directly. Never in history have we had such access to the thoughts of presidents, CEOs and captains of industry. Barack Obama, Rupert Murdoch and Richard Branson are all active on Twitter.

Have you got your smartphone with you right now? If you're at your computer, or have your phone accessible, open up search.twitter.com and do a search for mentions of your company name and your own name. You will see in real time what is being said about you. Did anything interesting come up? Tweet us if it did. We're on @Franklin_Adam and @Toby_Jenkins.

When Dave Kerpen tried this activity during a keynote to hundreds of CEOs at the Fortune Growth Summit, one CEO discovered that his company had just been mentioned favourably by a US Senator.

If you're still not sold on the power of this platform, please read on.

Twitter explained: for beginners

If you're completely new to Twitter, think of it as a giant room where lots of different people are chatting. A tweet is like a speech bubble, and you've got up to 140 characters to say what you want.

If people like what you have to say they may choose to follow you, and this means your tweets will show up in their newsfeed. You can also link to anywhere on the web, so it's a handy way to direct people to your blog. If you are both following each other, you can exchange direct messages (known as DMs), which are private, like text messages. (See the Twitter cheat sheet in figure 19.1 for more on common terminology.)

If someone is speaking to you, they will mention your Twitter handle (ours are @Toby_Jenkins and @Franklin_Adam). If you start your tweet with the @ symbol of a Twitter handle, your tweet will appear only in that person's Twitter feed or in the feed of anyone who follows you both. This is good news, as it means you can be very social on Twitter and not worry about cluttering up people's feeds.

Figure 19.1: Twitter cheat sheet

@Bluewire_Media	This is a username, commonly known as a 'Twitter handle'.
#hashtag	A hashtag indicates a subject or topic you are talking about
DM	'Direct Message'. Designed for private conversations, like a text message.
Tweet	This is your 140-character update.
RT	'ReTweet'. When you share someone else's tweet you can recognise them as the original tweeter with RT and their Twitter handle.
Trending	These are the most popular hashtags at any moment.
List	Lists are a way to categorise the people you follow.

Download the Twitter Cheat Sheet from www.bluewiremedia.com.au/twitter-cheat-sheet.

Twitter automatically shortens URLs, so you don't need to worry about burning up your 140 characters with a long web address. You may prefer to use bit.ly to shorten your URLs since it provides analytics such as how many times a link has been clicked.

How do I attract followers?

This is usually the first question on everyone's lips. Everyone wants friends, so getting your initial followers is quite important. When in doubt always relate it to real-life etiquette. Imagine walking into a room full of people you don't know. If you're an extrovert you'll most likely go and introduce yourself to some; if you're a bit more shy, you'll wait and listen in on a conversation for a while before chiming in. The same goes for Twitter.

Start by listening to who's talking about things you're interested in, then lean in and ask a question.

On Twitter, start by retweeting other people's tweets and maybe dropping in a comment.

> ### Pro Tip: @mention
>
> Always @mention people whose work you are sharing. It's good manners and a great way to share the love.

For example, the following tweet is a friendly, non-intrusive way to thank Toby for sharing an article. This technique is much better than clicking the retweet button because it allows you to personalise a message, which Adam has put in brackets.

Adam Franklin 🐦
@Franklin_Adam
(Great read, thanks!) RT @Toby_Jenkins: The shared genius of
Elon Musk and Steve Jobs buff.ly/1jqlkpp
25 Nov

Put your Twitter handle on everything

If you want more followers, include your Twitter handle in your email signature and business cards, and embed the Twitter widget on your website or blog, so you make it easy for people to follow you.

If you're building your email subscriber list, you can add a call-to-action on your newsletter asking your readers to follow you. If you have clients or colleagues who you know are on Twitter, search for them and tweet them. Interested people will follow you and you'll be growing your network.

Be social, don't 'do' social

The best rule of thumb for getting more followers is to interact with people and tweet lots of great content, both your own and other people's.

If you do interesting things, people will follow and retweet you.

When you start personal conversations and you are genuinely interested in what the other person is saying, you'll build your level of interactions and your number of followers will grow.

Can I fast-track this?

There are no shortcuts, but you can go to Tweepz to help find interesting people to follow. You can search for specific kinds of people and kick things off.

For example, our ideal buyer is a 'Sydney marketing manager'. A simple search on Tweepz shows all the people on Twitter who fit this criterion. We can even sort them by how many followers they have and by how long they've been on Twitter.

Do you recognise these common mistakes?

There are behaviours that should be actively avoided in Twitter land. These include:

1. Following people, and immediately hitting 'un-follow' once they follow you

This is as uncool as it gets. You are using and abusing people to boost your follower numbers artificially. It's no way to make friends, and is a dangerously silly trap to fall into.

2. Buying fake followers

If you had imaginary friends in real life, people would probably look at you funny or maybe ridicule you. On Twitter it's even worse, because you'll reek of desperation and erode any trust you may have built up. You put your entire credibility and reputation on the line if you buy followers. It's a bad look, and of course they're never going to share your content. If you are even the slightest bit tempted, stop.

Focus on connecting with real people, as in real life.

3. Flogging your products and talking about yourself

It is possible to make sales via Twitter but it isn't the place to be spruiking yourself. Michael Hyatt, author of *Platform*, recommends treating Twitter like a 'social bank account'. You definitely can make 'withdrawals' but you need to have invested in your community first. A good rule of thumb is to aim for a 20-to-1 ratio. Only once you've shared helpful content, interacted with people and added value 20 times, should you consider asking for help or touting a product.

4. Aggressive following

People commonly go on a 'following rampage' when they open their Twitter account. There are two reasons why this is a bad idea. Firstly, people won't trust you much if you have only a handful of followers but follow hundreds of people. Unfortunately this looks a bit desperate too, like the guy slinging business cards around at a networking event. Or worse still, people may assume you are boring because few people are following you.

Secondly, Twitter might actually suspend your account if you follow people aggressively, because that's what spammers do. A good rule of thumb is to keep your following-to-followers ratio at 40:60 or, at the very least, keep the numbers equal.

Should I 'un-follow' people who aren't adding value?

Sure. If you've got time to kill and you want go through and reassess the people you follow, feel free to. Don't stress that you might upset anyone either—they are probably too busy to notice. However, culling followers is usually a sign that you're procrastinating, so unless you really have to, take a look at what you *should* be doing instead.

Remember, it's not a race to get the most followers; it's an opportunity to connect with real people and participate in a community.

Twitter marketing in 5 minutes a day

- Tweet some content of your own (1 minute).

- Scan your feed and share an interesting tweet from someone else—remember to include their @twitter_handle (2 minutes).

- Check your @mentions and interact by saying thanks (2 minutes).

Twitter tools to use

Here are some essential tools for Twitter users:

- *Twitter app*. Never feel cut off from your news. Twitter is a very easy application for your smartphone, so you can take it with you and check it on the go. The app is perfect for those dead times when you'd be twiddling your thumbs, like waiting at the airport or commuting on a train or bus. Even when waiting for a meeting you can use the time productively by sending a few tweets.

- *Buffer*. If you're like us you probably have better things to be doing than logging onto Twitter every 20 minutes. Scheduling tweets in advance becomes really easy with Buffer's free app.

- *Topsy*. Topsy keeps an archive of every single tweet published since 2006. You can search for all those classic tweets that were so hard to find on Twitter.

- *HootSuite*. With this free tool you can connect to Twitter (and your other social networks) and set up streams to track all your @ mentions, direct mentions (DMs) and any hashtags you are interested in. The bonus is you can also set up a stream to follow keywords that your buyers might be searching.

- *Bit.ly*. This is a free URL shortening tool that has the added benefit of analytics.

Intermediate Twitter

Once you are following over a hundred or so people, it becomes easy to lose track of people's tweets. This is where Twitter's list functionality comes in.

Lists

Twitter allows you to segment the people you follow into separate, easy-to-manage lists. Adam follows a list of his 'favourite bloggers' and also 'journalists' who cover the industry, but you can organise it however you like.

On your profile page, you can go to Lists, Create list, name it, save it and Add people to it.

Pro Tip: Click to tweet.

You'll have noticed that when you read some blogs and email newsletters, they have a nifty 'tweet this' link. If you've ever wondered how to do that, Clicktotweet.com will give you the answer. (We incorporate this tool in our Bluewire News emails, in our blog posts and also on the Thank you/Download pages of our premium content landing pages.) This way you can build sharing into your marketing system, and it can run on autopilot.

Hashtags

Hashtags are a way of keeping track of certain topics that are being talked about. They are especially popular during events, live sports or TV shows because they allow people to comment and interact with each other about a shared interest. Even people who can't make the event, game or show can keep tabs on what's going on.

The example shown here features the hashtag #SMDU, which we used for our Social Media Down Under conference in Sydney.

Marc Lehmann 🐦
@marclehmann
Inspired to be Action Jackson today after soaking up awesome #SMDU speakers @TimboReid @rexter @valeriekhoo @CBadenach @trevoryoung
Jul 3

The following tweets are an example of people at the conference and all over the world, interacting with each other on the #SMDU stream.

Bluewire Media 🐦
@Bluewire_Media
The latest Bluewire News - all the slides, reports & podcast from Social Media Down Under #SMDU
bluewi.re/18vGd2v
Jul 20

Tony Hollingsworth 🐦
@hollingsworth
Hey @selina_power talking about you with simonleong Thanks for #smdu. When you back in Sydney? @ Beppi's
instagram.com/p/bkclVTDO9S/
Jul 9

Marc Lehmann 🐦
@marclehmann
Inspired to be Action Jackson today after soaking up awesome #SMDU speakers @TimboReid @rexter @valeriekhoo @CBadenach @trevoryoung
Jul 3

David Meerman Scott 🐦
@dmscott
@AskTonyIT How cool is that? Wish I had been there with you at #smdu @tristanjwhite
Jul 3

Tony Hollingsworth 🐦
@hollingsworth
Props @Bluewire_Media for a great event. @Selina_Power wraps it up #smdu @ Australian National ... instagram.com/p/bS23KcjO7S/
Jul 3

Pro Tip: Buy your own 'short domain' and map it to your Bit.ly account.

Then when you tweet, instead of showing http://bit.ly it will show your custom short link. For example, we use http://bluewi.re. Head over to http://domai.nr to see what domains are available.

Twitter for recruitment

Gone are the days when employers could attract staff with lame 'this is what it's like at our company' job descriptions. The same goes for relying on your inflated résumé. Employment—on both sides of the fence—has changed, and social media is responsible.

Previously employers would often gripe that the real 'A players' were seldom looking at job-listing websites because they were so well looked after in their roles, and likely subject to generous offers all the time anyway. So how are you to find the best talent, if they're never looking at your job ads?

The key is to get on their radar via social networks like Twitter. If you're an organisation that is contributing valuable information, resources and thought leadership to the industry via blogging, guest blogging, events, speaking and social media, you will be in a good position to gain the attention of the best people in the industry.

On the flip side, the best companies to work for often fill roles without advertising the position, and if they do list it, they're swamped with hundreds of applications from excellent candidates. How do you rise above the noise?

Not surprisingly, the answer again lies with social media, and with Twitter especially.

For employers and employees alike, if you're active on Twitter you can follow the best companies and people in your space. You can also share your own body of work, so you can make a name for yourself. Résumés still change hands, but increasingly people are turning to social media to validate applications. Your body of work online (and making it visible via Twitter) is such a big part of your digital résumé these days that to ignore it is downright dangerous for your career and business prospects.

Nearly all of the people we have employed over the years have been active on Twitter, and for us this has weighed heavily in their favour. Our presence on Twitter has made Bluewire Media more attractive to the candidates too. It's a logical thing for a web marketing and social media firm to do, and it's fast becoming commonplace across the business world as employers look to find and attract the best talent.

Who wants to work for a company that bans social media, or just doesn't get it? Who wants to hire someone, especially in a marketing role, junior or senior, who isn't on social media or, even more concerning, has made the decision to dismiss it? If your organisation rejects social media because they'd rather the team 'do real work' instead, we'd suggest this is a dangerous philosophy.

Leveraging Twitter across your organisation

Smart companies are realising that their teams are potentially the company's biggest and most vocal advocates. If they can provide the tools, training, and most importantly the 'permission' to embrace social media, then they can mobilise an army of supporters. Trust, empowerment and support are paramount.

Let's look at Deloitte again. Their social media policy has evolved to just three words: 'Trust and Empower'. Thousands of employees are free to interact with each other, with clients and with the sea of prospective clients on Twitter. This is all happening while many of their competitors are banning social networks and missing this opportunity.

Who is your money on for the next decade? Ours is on Deloitte and leaders like Giam Swiegers.

Advanced Twitter

Twitter Advanced Search is very useful if you are looking to discover things like whether people are tweeting positively or negatively.

Figure 19.2 shows some Advanced Search ideas that will help you narrow your search.

Figure 19.2: Twitter Advanced Search ideas

Bluewire Media	contains the exact phrase 'Bluewire Media'
Toby OR Adam	contains either the word 'Toby' or 'Adam'
Social –Media	contains 'social' but not 'media'
#Twitter	contains the hashtag #Twitter
near:Sydney within:15km	sent within 15 kilometres of Sydney
Website :(	contains 'website' and a negative face
Design :)	contains 'design' and a positive face
Help?	contains the word 'help' with a question mark

For more, check out the Twitter Cheat Sheet at www.bluewiremedia.com.au/twitter-cheat-sheet.

Twitter is an exciting tool offering plenty of marketing opportunities. Go ahead and tweet us @Franklin_Adam and @Toby_Jenkins—we look forward to tweeting you.

Pro Tip: Don't sell – find people looking for your products.

Say you run a bike shop in Sydney. Instead of blasting Twitter with special promotions on your bikes, use Twitter Advanced Search to find people talking about bikes around Sydney. This way you can listen to and join their conversations.

Summary

→ Twitter is a powerful platform for CEOs and marketers alike.

→ If you are a self-proclaimed 'digital dinosaur', recruit a 'digital native' to teach you social media.

→ Attract followers by promoting your Twitter handle, sharing great content and being active.

→ There are many intermediate and advanced tips you can use too.

Tools and templates

Twitter Cheat Sheet
www.bluewiremedia.com.au/twitter-cheat-sheet

Twitter 5 Minute Marketing Plan
www.bluewiremedia.com.au/twitter-marketing-plan

Topsy
www.topsy.com

HootSuite
www.hootsuite.com

Click to tweet
www.clicktotweet.com

Domai.nr
www.domai.nr

Twitter Search
https://search.twitter.com

Tweepz
www.tweepz.com

Buffer
www.bufferapp.com

Platform: Get Noticed In A Noisy World by Michael Hyatt
michaelhyatt.com/platform

Part VII

The future

Chapter 20

The road ahead

Action is the foundational key to all success.

Pablo Picasso

Picture yourself in three years' time. You open up your smartphone and discover another hundred people have downloaded your flagship content overnight. These people will now be able to get to know you through your regular newsletter and help themselves to your premium content. You smile and feel proud that you've been able to help all these people solve their problems.

Your recent blog post is already ranking on the first page of Google and is being shared and linked to by people all over the web. The comments section is on fire. Prospects are queuing up to do business with you and your products are selling well. Your web marketing asset is humming and your colleagues marvel at the results.

You reflect on just how far your marketing has come.

∽

As you implement the marketing framework we have introduced in this book, and make it your own, know that every step you take builds upon the last. Today everyone has an extraordinary opportunity to build a web marketing asset.

The tools and technology we now have access to can help people on a scale never before imagined. Technology will continue to change—the irony lies in the fact that as it does it will make our organisations *more human* than ever. Harnessing these tools boils down to just one thing: people.

Whatever your business, remember that it is *people* you are talking to, *people* who come to your website and read your blog, *people* you are tweeting with. Understanding who those people are—your buyer personas—is the first step. Once you have identified their problems, and how you can help, it is up to you to connect one with the other.

Your flagship content helps to bridge the gap between problem and solution. It's the piece of your marketing puzzle that enables people to get to know, like and trust you. By being generous online *and* offline, you'll build and nurture a community. With every valuable piece of content you can uncover, create and release, you'll build your marketing asset—one block at a time. Finally, you'll use social media to amplify your results, and empower your team to do the same.

We hope you find this framework and our downloadable templates valuable as you make this journey. We wish you every success and would love to hear how you go.

All the best,

Adam and Toby

adam.franklin@bluewiremedia.com.au

toby.jenkins@bluewiremedia.com.au

Index

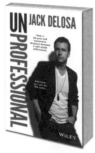